STUDY GUIDE

Financial Management and Policy

STUDY GUIDE

Irene Hammerbacher/Frank McGrath
Iona College

Ninth Edition

James C. Van Horne
Stanford University

Financial Management and Policy

Prentice Hall, Englewood Cliffs, New Jersey 07632

Editorial/production supervision: *Elaine Price*
Supplements acquisitions editor: *David Scholder*
Manufacturing buyers: *Trudy Pisciotti/Bob Anderson*

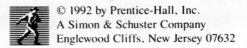
Printed in the United States of America

10 9 8 7 6 5 4 3 2 1

ISBN 0-13-322090-7

Prentice-Hall International (UK) Limited, *London*
Prentice-Hall of Australia Pty. Limited, *Sydney*
Prentice-Hall Canada Inc., *Toronto*
Prentice-Hall Hispanoamericana, S.A., *Mexico*
Prentice-Hall of India Private Limited, *New Delhi*
Prentice-Hall of Japan, Inc., *Tokyo*
Simon & Schuster Asia Pte. Ltd., *Singapore*
Editora Prentice-Hall do Brasil, Ltda., *Rio de Janeiro*

TABLE OF CONTENTS

STUDY GUIDE

Financial Management and Policy

CHAPTER 1

GOALS AND FUNCTIONS OF FINANCE

PERSPECTIVE

Finance has developed from economics into a separate field of study. The evolution has generally followed changes in the business environment from a descriptive approach to the current emphasis on decision making. Management's investment, financing, and dividend decisions directly impact the market value of the company's stock. Therefore, the principle of maximization of shareholder wealth provides a rational guide for optimal decision making.

CHAPTER OUTLINE

I. Corporate finance evolved from economics.
   A. In the early 1900s, it described the instruments, institutions and procedures of the money and capital markets.
   B. In the 1920s, much attention was paid to investment banking and securities, particularly common stock.
   C. During the 1930s, the emphasis shifted to liquidity, debt, regulation, bankruptcy and reorganizations.
   D. During the 1940s and early 1950s, finance was still largely descriptive, but some attention began to be paid to internal analysis, planning, and control of cash flows.
   E. Later in the 1950s, capital budgeting, present value concepts, valuation models, and dividend policy were considered in detail.
   F. The 1960s saw the development of portfolio theory and both theoretical and empirical investigation of the functioning of financial markets.
   G. The 1970s saw the evaluation of the relative merits of the capital asset pricing model and the arbitrage pricing model for valuing financial assets, and the development of the option pricing model.
   H. Studies in the 1980s concentrated on the issues of uncertainty, asymmetric information, and financial signaling.
   I. The highly speculative, deregulated, increasingly globalized finance of the 1990s is causing a reevaluation of the strategic and ethical role of the CFO.

II. Throughout the changing environment and evolution of finance, the objective of the firm has remained constant.
   A. The objective of the firm is to create value for its shareholders by maximizing the market price of the company's common stock.
   B. Other standards have been proposed as proper objectives for the company, but they all have some shortcomings.
      1. Maximization of total profits is not as important as maximizing earnings per share.
      2. Maximization of earnings per share ignores
         a. the timing and duration of expected earnings.
         b. the risk or uncertainty of the prospective earnings stream.
         c. dividends.
      3. Because criteria for social responsibility are not clearly defined, it is difficult to formulate a consistent objective involving social goals.
   C. Shareholders can be assured that management will make optimal decisions to maximize shareholder wealth only under certain conditions.
      1. Appropriate incentives such as stock options, bonuses, and perks are given, but they must be tied to managerial performance.
      2. Management must be monitored, which involves agency costs.

III. Stock price maximization involves three major decisions.
   A. Investment decisions must be evaluated in relation to their expected return and risk.
      1. They determine the total amount of assets held by a company.
      2. They determine the composition of assets.
      3. They determine the amount of business risk a firm experiences.
   B. Financing decisions determine the company's capital structure.
   C. The dividend decision involves the balancing of a dividend's impact on stock price against the opportunity cost of retained earnings lost.

MULTIPLE CHOICE QUESTIONS

1.1 Finance was originally considered a part of
    a. management.
    b. marketing.
    c. production.
    d. economics.

1.2 The evolution of finance has been influenced over time by
   a. the development of economic theory.
   b. changes in the economic environment.
   c. fluctuations in inflation rates.
   d. the proliferation of financial institutions.

1.3 Today's finance is primarily
   a. descriptive.
   b. static.
   c. analytical.
   d. institutional.

1.4 Modern financial management is primarily concerned with
   a. financial institutions.
   b. financial markets.
   c. financial decision making.
   d. financial consolidations.

1.5 Financial management involves making the following major decisions:
   a. dividends, investment, and financing.
   b. wealth, valuation, and dividends.
   c. valuation, financing, and dividends.
   d. wealth, financing, and investment.

1.6 The decision that determines the total amount of assets held by the firm is the
   a. growth decision.
   b. dividend decision.
   c. financing decision.
   d. investment decision.

1.7 The decision concerned with determining the best capital structure is called the
   a. growth decision.
   b. dividend decision.
   c. financing decision.
   d. investment decision.

1.8 The decision concerning the amount of earnings retained in the firm is the
   a. growth decision.
   b. dividend decision.
   c. financing decision.
   d. investment decision.

1.9 The objective of the firm is to maximize
   a. profit.
   b. earnings per share.
   c. shareholder wealth.
   d. management compensation.

1.10 Setting a corporate goal of maximization of earnings per share involves consideration of
a. the time value of money.
b. stock repurchases.
c. the uncertainty of future earnings.
d. future dividends.

ANSWERS

1.1	d	p.	2	1.6	d	pp.	8-9
1.2	b	pp.	2-3	1.7	c	p.	9
1.3	c	p.	6	1.8	b	pp.	9-10
1.4	c	pp.	5-6	1.9	c	p.	6
1.5	a	pp.	8-9	1.10	b	pp.	6-7

CHAPTER 2

CONCEPTS IN VALUATION

███

PERSPECTIVE

The mathematical concept underlying valuation is the time value of money. Calculations involving compound interest and terminal value flow into calculations involving discount rates and present value. These techniques are used to amortize a loan and to compute the internal rate of return on different types of securities.

Time value of money formulas can be used to calculate the market price or the yield on discount bonds, coupon bonds, or perpetuities such as preferred stock.

The time value of money is also incorporated into the basic dividend model, and the perpetual growth and phased growth models for common stock. These models are used to calculate the expected return on an investment in common stock.

The concept of risk, as measured by the standard deviation, is then introduced. Investors attempt to maximize their expected utility, which is a function of both expected return and risk.

CHAPTER OUTLINE

I. The concept of the "time value of money" is the concept that $1 received or paid sooner is worth more to us than $1 received or paid later.
   A. Compound interest is the amount that the lender earns on the original principal plus the accumulated interest.
      1. The calculation of compound interest is based on the following equation:
      $TV_n = X_0(1 + r)^n$, where
         TV_n = terminal value after n periods,
         X_0 = beginning dollar amount,
         r = compound interest rate per period,
         n = number of periods.
      2. For example, suppose $100 is invested in a savings account paying 12 percent interest per year, and kept there for 2 years. Using the equation, the terminal value of the account is calculated as:
      $TV_2 = \$100(1.12)^2 = \$125.44$.
      3. Since interest is being earned on interest, large values of n and r produce large terminal values.
      4. The concept involved applies to compound growth of any sort; it is not restricted to interest rates.

5

5. Compounding does not have to be annual. If compounding occurs m times a year, the equation is adjusted to:
$$TV_n = X_0(1 + r/m)^{mn}.$$
6. For example, if $100 is deposited in a savings account paying 12 percent interest a year, compounded quarterly, and kept there for 2 years, the terminal value of the account becomes:
$$TV_2 = \$100(1 + 0.12/4)^{4 \times 2}$$
$$= \$100(1.03)^8 = \$126.68.$$
7. The greater the frequency of compounding, the higher the terminal value.
8. As m approaches infinity, the term $(1+r/m)^{mn}$ approaches e^{rn} where $e = 2.71828$ and the equation for terminal value becomes:
$$TV_n = X_0 e^{rn}.$$
9. For example, if $100 is deposited in a savings account paying 12 percent interest a year, compounded continuously, and kept there for 2 years, the terminal value of the account becomes:
$$TV_2 = \$100(2.71828)^{0.12 \times 2} = \$127.12$$
B. Present value is the amount that must be invested today to receive a specific dollar amount in the future.
1. The interest rate in present value problems is called the discount rate because it reduces future cash flows.
2. The calculation of present value is based on the following equation:
$$PV = A_n/(1 + k)^n, \text{ where}$$
PV = present value in dollars,
A_n = cash flow at the end of period n,
k = discount rate per period,
n = number of time periods.
3. For example, suppose a security will be worth $1,000 at the end of 3 years. If its yield is 12 percent annually, its present value (current market price) can be calculated as:
$$PV = \$1,000/(1.12)^3 = \$711.78.$$
4. The calculation of present value is the reverse of compounding. The present value equation could also be written as:
$$X_0 = TV_n/(1 + r)^n.$$
5. Large values of n and k produce small present values.
6. When interest is compounded more than once a year, the formula for calculating present value must be revised to:
$$PV = A_n/(1 + k/m)^{mn}, \text{ where}$$
m = the number of times per year that interest is compounded,
k = the annual discount rate.
7. For example, suppose a security will be worth $1,000 at the end of 3 years. If its yield is 12 percent annually, compounded quarterly, its present value can be calculated as:

$$PV = \$1,000/(1.03)^{12} = \$701.40$$

8. The more frequent the compounding, the lower the present value.

C. Present value calculations are not limited to lump-sum amounts received or paid once in the future.

1. The present value of an uneven series of future cash flows is calculated according to the following equation:

$$PV = A_0 + A_1/(1+k) + A_2/(1+k)^2 + \ldots, \text{ or}$$

$$PV = \sum_{t=0}^{n} A_t/(1+k)^t.$$

2. For example, if a 10 percent rate of return is required on a security that will produce cash flows of $400 a year from now, $300 two years from now, and $200 three years from now, its present value will be:

$$PV = \$400/(1.10)^1 + \$300/(1.10)^2 + \$200/(1.10)^3$$
$$= \$363.64 + \$247.93 + \$150.38$$
$$= \$761.95$$

3. A series of even cash flows is called an annuity. The present value of an annuity is calculated according to the following equation:

$$PV = A_t \sum_{t=0}^{n} [1/(1+k)^t]$$

4. For example, if a 10 percent rate of return is required on a security that will produce cash flows of $300 a year for 3 years, starting a year from now, its present value will be:

$$PV = (\$300)[1/1.10 + 1/(1.10)^2 + 1/(1.10)^3]$$
$$= (\$300)(2.4869)$$
$$= \$746.07$$

5. An important use of present value concepts is in amortizing a loan, that is, in determining the equal period payments which embody both payment of interest and repayment of principal.

6. For example, suppose you borrow $10,000 at 8 percent to be repaid over the next four years. Equal installment payments are required at the end of each year, and these payments must be sufficient in amount to repay the $10,000 and give the lender 8 percent interest on the outstanding balance of the loan. To determine the amount of each payment, solve the following equation for the value of A:

$$\$10,000 = A \sum_{t=1}^{4} [1/(1.08)^t]$$
$$\$10,000 = 3.3121A$$
$$A = \$3,019.23$$

7. An amortization schedule can be prepared which shows the annual payment, interest, principal, and outstanding balance.

D. The internal rate of return or yield for an investment is the discount rate that equates the present value of the expected cash outflows with the present value of the expected cash inflows.
 1. To find the internal rate of return, solve the following equation for r:

$$0 = \sum_{t=0}^{n} [A_t/(1+r)^t].$$

 2. If the equation involves only an initial outflow and one lump-sum payment somewhere in the future, the IRR can be obtained from the present value table.
 3. If the equation involves an initial outflow and an even series of future cash inflows, the IRR can be obtained from the annuity table.
 4. If the equation involves an initial outflow and an uneven series of future cash inflows, then the IRR must be found by a trial-and-error method if done without electronic help.

II. A bond is a security which promises the securityholder repayment of a loan, plus interest, sometime in the future. The value of this security depends on the terms of the promise and the time value of money.
 A. The customary denomination of a bond is $1,000, although it is quoted as $100, and the customary interest payments are semiannual.
 1. A discount bond (also called a zero-coupon bond) is one for which the issuer promises to make a single payment at a specified future date.
 2. The present value of a zero-coupon bond is
$P = F/(1 + r/2)^{2n}$, where
    P = present market price of the bond,
    F = face or maturity value,
    r = yield to maturity,
    n = number of years to maturity.
 3. Given any three of these variables, one can solve for the fourth.
 4. A coupon bond pays semiannual interest plus face value at maturity.
 5. The present value of a coupon bond is

$$P = \sum_{t=1}^{2n} [(C/2)/(1+r/2)^t] + F/(1+r/2)^{2n},$$ where

    P = present market price of the bond,
    C = annual coupon payment,
    F = face or maturity value,
    r = yield to maturity,
    n = number of years to maturity.
 6. Given any four of these variables, one can solve for the fifth.

7. A perpetuity is a security which promises a fixed cash inflow to be paid at equal intervals forever. British consols and preferred stocks are perpetuities.
8. The present value of a perpetuity is
$P = A*/r$, where
   P = present market price of perpetuity,
   $A*$ = fixed annual payment,
   r = annual yield.
9. Given any two of these variables, one can solve for the third.
B. The duration of a bond represents the weighted average time to the interest and principal payments.
1. The equation for duration is
$$D = \{ \sum_{t=1}^{n} [(C_t t)/(1+r)^t]\}/V, \text{ where}$$
   D = number of years duration,
   C_t = interest and/or principal payment at time t,
   t = number of years to that payment,
   n = number of years to maturity,
   r = yield to maturity,
   V = value or market price of bond.
2. For example, a 6 percent bond with 3 years to maturity has a current market price of $900. If its yield to maturity is 10 percent, then its duration is
$$D = [(60)(1)/(1.10) + (60)(2)/(1.10)^2 + (1060)(3)/(1.10)^3]/900$$
$$= (54.55 + 99.17 + 2389.18)/900$$
$$= 2.83 \text{ years}$$
3. The longer the duration of a debt instrument, the greater its price volatility with respect to changes in market interest rates.
4. For the bond in B.2., above, a 1 percent increase in interest rates would cause a 2.83 percent decrease in the price of the bond (from $900 to $874.53).

III. The market value of a share of common stock is not related to par value, book value, or liquidating value. It is related to the cash distribution to shareholders, which we call dividends.
A. The simplest stock valuation model is the perpetual growth model.
1. If dividends are expected to grow perpetually at a compound rate of g, then
$P_0 = D_1/(r-g)$, where
   P_0 = current market price of one share,
   D_1 = dividend per share at time 1,
   r = expected return to the shareholder,
   g = perpetual compound rate of dividend growth,
   and $r > g$.

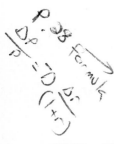

2. If a company retained a constant portion, b, of its earning every year, then the price earnings ratio should be

$P_0/E_1 = (1-b)/(r-g)$, where

E_1 = expected earnings in period 1,

$(1-b)$ = constant dividend payout ratio.

3. For most companies, a perpetual growth model is unrealistic.

B. A multiphase growth model may be more realistic.

1. A three-phase model assuming that dividends would grow at 15 percent for 5 years, 10 percent for the next 5 years, and 5 percent thereafter, would have the following share price equation:

$$P_0 = \sum_{t=1}^{5} [D_0(1.15)^t/(1+r)^t]$$

$$+ \sum_{t=6}^{10} [D_5(1.10)^{t-5}/(1+r)^t]$$

$$+ \sum_{t=11}^{\infty} [D_{10}(1.05)^{t-10}/(1+r)^t].$$

2. Since the solution of such an equation for r can be arduous, and the accuracy of the estimate depends on the quality of the forecasts, a quick and reasonably accurate approximation of the three-phase model has been developed.

3. The H model approximates the required return of a three-phase model as:

$r = (D_0/P_0)[(1+g_3) + H(g_1-g_3)] + g_3$, where

D_0 = present dividend per share,

P_0 = present market price per share,

g_3 = growth rate of dividends in third (final) phase,

H = (A+B)/2, where

A = number of years in first phase,

B = year at end of second phase,

g_1 = growth rate of dividends in first phase.

4. The H model is most useful when B is relatively small, $r > g_1$, and g_2 is about half way between g_1 and g_3. The further a situation is from these conditions, the poorer the approximation.

IV. Risk is the possibility that the actual return from holding a security will deviate from the expected return.

A. The expected return and risk of an investment can be measured as the mean and standard deviation of the probability distribution of possible returns from an investment.

1. The expected return is given by the equation:

$$E(R) = \sum_{i=1}^{n} R_i P_i, \text{ where}$$

R_i = the ith possible return,
P_i = the probability of occurrence of that return,
n = the total number of possible returns.

2. For example, suppose a particular investment has a 0.25 chance of returning 8 percent, a 0.50 chance of returning 3 percent, and a 0.25 chance of returning -2 percent. The expected return would be:

$$E(R) = (0.25)(0.08) + (0.5)(0.03) + (0.25)(-0.02)$$
$$= 0.02 + 0.015 - 0.005$$
$$= 0.03, \text{ or } 3\%.$$

3. The standard deviation is given by the equation:

$$\sigma = \left\{ \sum_{i=1}^{n} [R_i - E(R)]^2 P_i \right\}^{1/2}$$

4. For the investment example in A.2., above,

$$\sigma = [(0.08 - 0.03)^2(0.25) + (0.03 - 0.03)^2(0.50)$$
$$+ (-0.02 - 0.03)^2(0.25)]^{1/2}$$
$$= (0.00125)^{1/2}$$
$$= 0.354$$

5. The above example is a discrete probability distribution, so the probability that the actual return will be less than zero is 0.25.

6. If we had a continuous probability distribution with $E(R) = 3\%$ and $\sigma = 3.54\%$, we would have to standardize the deviation from the expected value:

$$0.03/0.0354 = 0.85\sigma$$

and then use the normal distribution table to find that the probability that the actual return will be less than zero is 19.77 percent.

B. For a risk-averse investor, utility increases at a decreasing rate with successive increments in wealth.
   1. The greater the risk (σ), the less the expected utility of an investment.
   2. The greater the risk, the less desirable it becomes.

MULTIPLE CHOICE QUESTIONS

2.1 Which of the following does not express the compound interest relationship?
   a. $TV = PV(1 + r)^n$
   b. $PV = TV(1 + k)^n$
   c. $r = (TV/PV)^{1/n} - 1$
   d. $PV = TV/(1 + k)^n$

2.2 You deposit funds today in an account which pays interest. If you wish to accumulate $100,000 in the account in 5 years, which of the following interest payment procedures will require the largest investment today?
   a. 5 percent, compounded annually
   b. 5 percent, compounded monthly
   c. 6 percent, compounded annually
   d. 6 percent, compounded monthly

2.3   You anticipate needing $80,000 in 18 years to send your brand-new first-born to college. The most conservative investment available pays 7 percent, compounded annually. How much must you invest today to meet that need?
a. $28,024
b. $25,112
c. $23,672
d. $20,016

2.4   You anticipate needing $80,000 in 18 years to send your brand-new second-born to college. The most conservative investment available pays 7 percent, compounded annually. How much must you invest annually to meet that need if you make the first investment today and the last at the end of year 17?
a. $1,902
b. $2,353
c. $2,444
d. $2,594

2.5   You anticipate needing $80,000 in 18 years to send your brand-new last-born to college. A reasonably conservative investment pays 7 percent, compounded continuously. How much must you convince the doting grandparents to invest today to meet that need?
a. $18,010
b. $22,467
c. $22,692
d. $22,920

2.6   You are considering buying a security that will give you $1,000 income each year for 5 years and can be liquidated at the end of the 5th year for $20,000. If your discount rate is 8 percent, how much is this investment worth to you today?
a. $3,993
b. $13,612
c. $17,605
d. $25,000

2.7   Suppose you borrow $50,000 at 10 percent, to be amortized over the next 10 years with a payment at the end of each year. How large must the payment be?
a. $8,137
b. $7,291
c. $6,978
d. $6,333

2.8   The internal rate of return is the rate that makes
a. the present value of the inflows equal zero.
b. the terminal value of the inflows equal zero.
c. the present value of the inflows equal the present value of the outflows.
d. the present value of the inflows equal the terminal value.

2.9   Pressco, Inc. issues a zero coupon bond with a face value of
      $1,000 and a maturity of 15 years. If the yield is 12 percent
      compounded semiannually, then the current market price is
      a. $233.
      b. $174.
      c. $131.
      d. $97.

2.10 ChocoCorp has a 12 percent, $100 face value preferred stock
      outstanding and the appropriate yield in today's market is 10
      percent. Its current market price should be
      a. $83.
      b. $100.
      c. $120.
      d. $150.

2.11 For coupon bonds, duration is _____ maturity.
      a. greater than
      b. the same as
      c. less than
      d. twice

2.12 The profit on an investment in stock is composed of
      a. dividends and the selling price of the stock.
      b. interest and dividends.
      c. capital gains and interest.
      d. capital gains and dividends.

2.13 Suppose you purchase a share of stock for $100 today. You
      hold the stock for one year and receive dividends of $4 at the
      end of the year. Immediately upon receiving the dividends,
      you sell the stock for $108. What is the rate of return on
      your investment in the stock?
      a. 4 percent
      b. 6 percent
      c. 8 percent
      d. 12 percent

2.14 EAP Corp. has the following possible returns: 3 percent, 6
      percent, and 9 percent. The probabilities associated with
      these returns are 0.3, 0.4, and 0.3, respectively. What is
      the standard deviation of the returns?
      a. 2.3 percent
      b. 3.0 percent
      c. 4.5 percent
      d. 4.9 percent

ANSWERS

2.1 b pp. 13-14

2.2 a pp. 21-22

2.3 c pp. 17-18   Use Table D: 7% and 18 years
                     ($80,000)(0.2959) = $23,672

2.4 b pp. 18-19   Use Table B: 7% and 18 years
                     $80,000/33.999 = $2,353.01

2.5 c p. 22   Use Table C: (.07)(18) = 1.26
                     $80,000/3.525418 = $22,692

2.6 c pp. 22-23   Use Tables D & E: 8% and 5 years
                     ($1,000)(3.9927) + ($20,000)(0.6806) =
                     $17,604.70

2.7 a p. 20   Use Table E: 10% and 10 years
                     $50,000/6.1446 = $8,137.23

2.8 c p. 22

2.9 b pp. 24-25   Use Table D: 6% and 30 periods
                     ($1,000)(0.1741) = $174.10

2.10 c pp. 26-27   [($100)(0.12)]/.10 = $120

2.11 c p. 25

2.12 d p. 29

2.13 d pp. 30-31   [($108 - $100) + $4]/$100 = 12%

2.14 a pp. 39-40   Mean return = (3%)(.3) + (6%)(.4) + (9%)(.3)
                            = 6%
                     $\sigma = [(3\% - 6\%)^2(.3) + (6\% - 6\%)^2(.4)$
                        $+ (9\% - 6\%)^2(.3)]^{1/2}$
                       = 2.3%

CHAPTER 3

MARKET RISK AND RETURNS

██

PERSPECTIVE

Since security prices in efficient capital markets fully reflect all available information, arbitrage opportunities are absent.

The return on a portfolio of securities is a weighted average of the individual securities' returns, but the risk of a portfolio is a function of both the standard deviations of the individual securities and the correlation of their possible returns. By diversifying a portfolio to include securities that are not perfectly correlated with each other, risk can be reduced relative to expected return.

The total risk of a security can be divided into systematic and unsystematic components. Systematic risk affects all securities and cannot be diversified away. Unsystematic risk is unique to a particular security and can be eliminated with efficient diversification. The Capital Asset Pricing Model describes the relationship between systematic risk and expected return.

CHAPTER OUTLINE

I. If a market is efficient, it uses all available information in setting a price.
   A. New information can rapidly change the intrinsic value of a security, but subsequent price movements will not follow any pattern.
   B. There are three forms of market efficiency.
      1. The weak-form means that an unanticipated return is not correlated with previous unanticipated returns.
      2. The semistrong form means that an unanticipated return is not correlated with any publicly available information.
      3. The strong form means that an unanticipated return is not correlated with either publicly available or insider information.
   C. Evidence tends to support the conclusion that the stock market, particularly the NYSE, is semistrong efficient, although market imperfections can exist.
   D. An arbitrage opportunity means finding two things that are essentially the same, but priced differently. An arbitrager will buy the cheaper item and sell (or sell

15

short) the more expensive item. Arbitrage actions equalize the prices.
  E. Therefore an efficient market is characterized by the absence of arbitrage opportunities.

II. A portfolio consists of two or more securities.
  A. The expected return on a portfolio is calculated as the weighted average of the expected returns of all the securities in the portfolio:

$$r_p = \sum_{j=1}^{m} r_j A_j, \text{ where}$$

   r_p = expected return on the portfolio,
   r_j = expected return on security j,
   A_j = proportion of portfolio funds invested in security j,
   m = number of securities in the portfolio.
  B. The risk of a portfolio is calculated as the standard deviation of a probability distribution of possible portfolio returns:

$$\sigma_p = (\sum_{j=1}^{m} \sum_{k=1}^{m} A_j A_k \sigma_{jk})^{1/2}, \text{ where}$$

   σ_p = risk of the portfolio,
   $\sigma_{jk} = r_{jk}\sigma_j\sigma_k$ = the covariance between possible returns for securities j and k,
   r_{jk} = expected correlation between possible returns for securities j and k,
   σ_j = standard deviation for security j.
  C. For example, suppose in a two-security portfolio, the first security has $r_1 = 10\%$ and $\sigma_1 = 2\%$, the second security has $r_2 = 8\%$ and $\sigma_2 = 4\%$. If the portfolio contains equal dollar investments in the two securities and $r_{12} = .35$, then

   $r_p = (1/2)(10\%) + (1/2)(8\%)$
   $\quad = 9\%$
   $\sigma_p = [(1/2)^2(2\%)^2 + (1/2)^2(4\%)^2$
   $\quad + (2)(1/2)(1/2)(.35)(2\%)(4\%)]^{1/2}$
   $\quad = 2.53\%$
  D. The difference between 2.53 percent and 3 percent (a weighted average of the standard deviations of the two securities) is called the diversification effect.
  E. When portfolio risk and return (X and Y) are graphed for all possible weights of the two securities within that portfolio, the resultant curve is known as the opportunity set.
    1. If the straight line connecting the points ($A_1 = 1$, $A_2 = 0$) and ($A_1 = 0$, $A_2 = 1$) were drawn, the spread between this line and the opportunity set represents the diversification effect.
    2. The opportunity set may bend backwards.
    3. The point furthest to the left on the opportunity set is known as the minimum variance (least risky) portfolio.

16

4. The efficient set is that portion of the opportunity set curve going from the minimum variance portfolio to the maximum expected return portfolio (the highest point on the curve).
5. As the correlation between the returns on the securities decreases, the opportunity set is pulled to the left, although the two end points do not change.

F. For a portfolio containing more than two securities, the same principles hold, but the opportunity set is an area instead of a line.
1. The efficient set (also called the "efficient frontier") lies on the highest line connecting the minimum variance portfolio and the maximum expected return portfolio.
2. Portfolios below and to the right of the efficient set are dominated by portfolios on the efficient set; investors should seek dominant portfolios.
3. Individual investors' choices of a specific portfolio will depend on their degree of risk aversion; i.e., the acceptable trade-off between risk and return.

G. If a risk-free security exists, and both borrowing and lending are possible at that rate, the market portfolio dominates all others.
1. The market portfolio is a portfolio of all securities available in the market, weighted by their respective total market values.
2. The separation theorem states that the determination of an optimal portfolio of risky assets is independent of the individual's risk preference.
3. The individual need only determine the most desirable combination of the risk-free security and the market portfolio.

H. The diversification effect is enhanced by international investment. The outer edge of the global opportunity set is to the left of the opportunity set for all U.S. stocks.
1. During the 1970s and 1980s, non-U.S. stocks averaged both a higher return and a larger standard deviation than U.S. stocks.
2. Exchange rate risks and the lack of synchronized economic cycles add to the global diversification effect.

III. The Capital Asset Pricing Model (CAPM) states that, in market equilibrium, a security will be expected to provide a return commensurate with that portion of its risk which cannot be avoided by diversification.
A. CAPM is built on a set of assumptions.
1. Capital markets are highly efficient.
2. Transactions costs are zero.
3. There are negligible restrictions on investment.
4. There are no taxes.
5. Investors are well informed, in general agreement about their expectations for individual securities, plan a

common holding period, and are individually too small to affect the market price of a stock.

B. Treasury securities are considered to fit the definition of a "risk-free security whose return over the holding period is known with certainty."

C. Standard and Poor's 500 Stock Index (or a broader index) can be a surrogate for the market portfolio.

D. Excess return can be calculated from historical data or from analysts' future estimates, and is defined as

$R_E = (P_1 - P_0 + D)/P_0 - R_f$, where

R_E = excess return for a security or portfolio,
P_0 = price at beginning of period,
P_1 = price at end of period,
D = dividends paid during period,
R_f = risk-free rate of return.

E. When excess returns for the market portfolio and for an individual stock are graphed over time, a line fitted to the data is called the characteristic line for that stock.

1. It is expected to have an intercept ("alpha") of zero and a positive slope ("beta").

2. If beta = 1.0, the stock has the same unavoidable or systematic risk as the market.

3. The beta of a stock represents its contribution to the risk of a highly diversified portfolio of stocks.

4. Betas are computed and published for actively traded stocks by a number of financial organizations.

5. Beta can be calculated as a measure of relative systematic risk by using the equation:

$\beta_j = r_{jm}\sigma_j/\sigma_m$, where

β_j = beta for security j,
r_{jm} = expected correlation between possible returns for security j and the market portfolio,
σ_j = standard deviation of the probability distribution of possible returns for security j,
σ_m = standard deviation of the probability distribution of possible returns for the market portfolio.

F. Unsystematic risk can be avoided; it is unique to a particular company and independent of economic, political, and other factors that affect securities in a systematic manner.

1. Unsystematic risk can be reduced by adding more stocks to a portfolio. This reduction occurs at a decreasing rate as more stocks are added.

2. Unsystematic risk = $1 - r_{jm}$.

3. The CAPM assumes all unsystematic risk has been diversified away.

G. In market equilibrium, the relationship between an individual security's expected rate of return and its systematic risk (beta) will be a straight line, called the security market line (SML).

18

1. The risk-free rate is the intercept of the line.
2. One point on the line is the expected rate of return on the market portfolio and $\beta = 1$.
3. Under the assumptions of CAPM, all securities are points on the SML.
4. The investor in a single security will be exposed to both systematic and unsystematic risk, but will be rewarded for only the systematic risk that is borne.
5. If an individual security has an expected return-risk combination that places it above the SML, it will be undervalued in the market. If it is below the SML, it will be overvalued.

IV. There are many caveats accompanying the use of CAPM.
   A. There is disagreement about the appropriate market risk premium, $\bar{R}_m - R_f$.
      1. The expected market risk premium has ranged from 3 percent to 7 percent in recent years.
      2. The historical market risk premium from 1926 to 1988 is 8.4 percent if calculated arithmetically and 6.2 percent if calculated geometrically.
      3. The average risk-free rate from 1926 to 1988 was only 3.6 percent.
      4. There is controversy over the use of a short-, intermediate- or long-term Treasury security.
      5. Expected returns are not necessarily actual or realized returns.
   B. The investor probably cannot both lend and borrow at the risk-free rate, as originally assumed.
      1. This implies that there is probably more than one optimal portfolio in the efficient set.
      2. An alternative solution requires the construction of a zero-beta portfolio, estimation of the zero-beta SML, and a zero-beta return to replace R_f.
      3. This zero-beta SML is sometimes referred to as the empirical SML.
   C. If investors' expectations are not homogeneous, only rough estimates of the expected return-risk tradeoffs for portfolios and individual securities are possible.
   D. Transactions costs and minimum transaction sizes may create bands on either side of the efficient set, within which investors' portfolios would lie.
   E. The "true" market portfolio consists of all assets: stocks, bonds, real estate and human capital.
   F. A stock's beta shows considerable variation depending upon which proxy market index is used.

MULTIPLE CHOICE QUESTIONS

3.1 The weak form of market efficiency means that an unanticipated return is not correlated with
   a. the Dow Jones Industrial Avel ̗e.
   b. previous unanticipated returns.
   c. any publicly available informatio...
   d. either publicly available or insider information.

3.2 When portfolio risk and expected return are graphed for all possible weights of two securities, the resultant curve is known as
   a. the opportunity set.
   b. the characteristic line.
   c. the security market line.
   d. the CAPM.

3.3 The risk of a well diversified portfolio will never be _____ the weighted average of the standard deviations of its component securities.
   a. half of
   b. less than
   c. equal to
   d. more than

3.4 Theoretically, the market portfolio includes
   a. common stock but not preferred stock.
   b. stock but not bonds.
   c. all securities available in the market.
   d. only high-quality stocks and bonds.

3.5 The diversification effect is enhanced by
   a. adding more money to a portfolio.
   b. high risk-free rates.
   c. global investment.
   d. avoiding exchange rate risks.

3.6 The intercept of the characteristic line is
   a. alpha.
   b. beta.
   c. the market risk premium.
   d. the risk-free rate.

3.7 The slope of the characteristic line is
   a. alpha.
   b. beta.
   c. the market risk premium.
   d. the risk-free rate.

3.8 The intercept of the Security Market Line is
   a. alpha.
   b. beta.
   c. the market risk premium.
   d. the risk-free rate.

3.9 Beta is a measure of
   a. systematic risk.
   b. unsystematic risk.
   c. diversifiable risk.
   d. total risk.

3.10 Assume that the beta of the Charlemagne Champagne Corp. has been calculated as 1.6. If the excess returns on the Standard and Poor's 500 Stock Index are expected to be 2 percent, then the excess returns on CCC are expected to be
   a. 0.8 percent.
   b. 3.2 percent.
   c. 8.0 percent.
   d. 32.0 percent.

ANSWERS

3.1	b	p.	52	3.6	a	pp.	65-66
3.2	a	p.	59	3.7	b	pp.	66-67
3.3	d	p.	58	3.8	d	p.	73
3.4	c	pp.	61-62	3.9	a	pp.	66-67
3.5	c	p.	63	3.10	b	p.	67

CHAPTER 4

MULTI VARIABLE AND FACTOR VALUATION

PERSPECTIVE

The CAPM may be expanded to include variables besides beta, such as tax policy, inflation, liquidity, size, the price-earnings ratio, and seasonal and industry effects. These variables tend to increase the explanatory power of the CAPM.

Factor models relate expected returns to multiple risks. The factors employed may be either theoretically specified or developed as results of empirical analysis, but they are intended to capture unavoidable risk. Factor models then relate unanticipated changes in the factors to the expected returns on individual securities.

The arbitrage pricing theory (APT) is an equilibrium model based on the use of arbitrage to eliminate inefficiencies created by various risk factors. As a result, arbitragers make the market efficient.

CHAPTER OUTLINE

I. The CAPM is a single factor model relating the expected return on a security to beta, a reaction coefficient to the overall market.
   A. There may be a systematic bias in the market in favor of capital gains and against dividends.
      1. Capital gains may be taxed at a more favorable rate than dividends in some states and periodically by the federal government.
      2. The present value of the tax on capital gains when realized may be less than the present value of the annual tax on dividends.
      3. If a preference for capital gains over dividends exists, the CAPM equation should be extended to
         $\overline{R}_j = R_f + b\beta_j + t(d_j - R_f)$, where
         $\overline{R}_j$ = expected before-tax return on security j,
         R_f = risk-free rate,
         b = coefficient of beta,
         β_j = beta for security j,
         t = coefficient of dividend yield,
         d_j = dividend yield on security j.
      4. The relative sizes of b and t would indicate the relative importance of the market and the tax effects, respectively.

B. Investors are generally believed to be concerned with inflation when making investment decisions.
   1. If inflation is predictable with a great deal of accuracy, investors will simply add an inflation premium to the real return they require.
   2. If inflation is uncertain, the consequences of unanticipated changes in the rate of inflation must be considered.
      a. If the return on a stock increases with the unanticipated increases in inflation, the systematic risk of the stock in real terms is reduced.
      b. If a stock's return goes down with unanticipated increases in inflation, the systematic risk of the stock in real terms is increased.
   3. One might expand the CAPM equation to
      $\overline{R}_j = R_f + b\beta_j - i(\sigma_{Ri}/\sigma_i^2)$, where
      σ_{Ri} = covariance of security j's expected return with unanticipated changes in inflation,
      σ_i^2 = variance of inflation,
      i = coefficient of relative inflation sensitivity.
   4. Empirical models tend to show no increased predictive power over beta-only models.
C. Low P/E stocks tend to earn more than the rate predicted by CAPM and high P/E stocks tend to earn less than the rate predicted.
   1. The price-earnings ratio has been included in the CAPM in a number of ways, and has been found to be statistically significant.
   2. One form of this CAPM extension is
      $\overline{R}_j = R_f + b\beta_j - p(P/E_j - P/E_m)$, where
      P/E_j = price-earnings ratio for security j,
      P/E_m = price-earnings ratio for the market portfolio,
      p = price-earnings coefficient.
D. Other variables have been added to the CAPM.
   1. Liquidity is the ability to sell a security quickly and without significant price concession. Investors presumably prefer high to low liquidity.
   2. Size can be measured by the relative market capitalization of a company. A "small stock effect" has been recognized, where small capitalization stocks provide a higher return than large capitalization stocks.
   3. Seasonal effects have to do with the month and/or the day of the week in which a security trade takes place. The "January effect" is an example of this.
   4. Attempts have been made to isolate industry effects by using dummy variables to categorize the particular industry in which a company primarily operates.
E. When one or more variables are added to the CAPM equation containing beta, a better data fit is generally obtained. But beta still remains the dominant determinant of security returns.

II. Factor models suggest that expected returns are affected by a number of risks. These models involve various economic variables, but not necessarily beta.
   A. The actual return on a security can be explained by the generalized factor model:
   $R_j = a + b_{1j}F_1 + b_{2j}F_2 + \ldots + e_j$, where
      R_j = actual return on security j,
      a = R_j when all factors have zero value,
      F_n = the uncertain value of factor n,
      b_{nj} = coefficient measuring reaction of R_j to a one-unit change in factor n,
      e_j = error term for security j, which measures unsystematic risk.
   B. Every factor has an anticipated and an unanticipated component, and it is the latter which causes security prices to change. This surprise element constitutes risk and is undiversifiable, or unavoidable.
   C. The expected return on a security is expressed by the equation:
   $E(\overline{R}_j) = \lambda_0 + \lambda_1 b_{1j} + \lambda_2 b_{2j} + \ldots$, where
      λ_0 = return on a risk-free asset,
      λ_i = risk premium for the surprise element in F_i,
      b_{ij} = reaction coefficient of security j to factor i.
   D. Factor models are based on the idea that security prices move together or apart in reaction to common forces, as well as randomly.

III. Arbitrage pricing theory (APT) is based on the idea that in competitive financial markets, arbitrage will ensure that riskless assets provide the same expected return. The prices of risky assets are driven to equilibrium by investors eliminating arbitrage profits caused by a limited number of factors.
   A. According to the APT, two securities with the same reaction coefficients (b_{ij}) should provide the same expected return. If they do not, several things will happen.
      1. Investors will buy the (underpriced) security with the higher expected return, driving the price up and the expected return down.
      2. Investors will sell, or sell short, the (overpriced) security with the lower expected return, driving the price down and the expected return up.
      3. This arbitrage process will continue until the expected returns are equalized.
   B. The Roll-Ross model suggests that there are five systematic factors that capture the major sources of security portfolio risk. The first three affect the cash flow of the company and the last two the market capitalization (discount) rate. The five factors are:
      1. changes in expected inflation,
      2. unanticipated changes in inflation,
      3. unanticipated changes in industrial production,

      4. unanticipated changes in the yield differential between
         low- and high-grade bonds,
      5. unanticipated changes in the yield differential between
         long-term and short-term bonds.
   C. Other empirical studies have employed different factors and
      disagreement abounds.

MULTIPLE CHOICE QUESTIONS

4.1 Taxes on dividend income and capital gains
     a. have been at an equal (federal) rate since the 1986 Tax
        Act.
     b. are the same in all 50 states.
     c. have the same present value.
     d. are due and payable at the same time.

4.2 If capital gains are preferred to dividends in the market as
     a whole, then CAPM can be extended by adding
     a. the investor's marginal tax rate.
     b. the stock's dividend yield.
     c. the market portfolio's after-tax expected return.
     d. the stock's dividend payout rate.

4.3 The realized real return for a security is a function of
     a. the inflation rate.
     b. inflation covariance.
     c. unanticipated changes in inflation.
     d. changes in expected inflation.

4.4 Other things being equal, security returns should be higher
     for stocks with
     a. high liquidity.
     b. large market capitalizations.
     c. low dividend yields.
     d. low price-earnings ratios.

4.5 A pattern of excess returns on investment is often exhibited
     in
     a. December.
     b. January.
     c. June.
     d. September.

4.6 In the extended CAPM equation, the coefficients reflect
     a. changes in the risk-free rate.
     b. the relative variability of the variable involved.
     c. the relative importance of the variable involved.
     d. everything except beta.

4.7 In factor models of specific securities, the error term represents
a. the return when all factors have zero value.
b. the uncertainties in the factors.
c. unsystematic risk.
d. systematic risk.

4.8 A factor model of the expected return on a security contains
a. the factor itself.
b. the expected component of the factor.
c. risk premiums for the types of risk associated with particular factors.
d. no more than two factors.

4.9 Suppose returns required in the market by investors are a function of two factors and a 6 percent risk-free rate, such that $E(\bar{R}_j) = 0.06 + 0.05b_{1j} + 0.08b_{2j}$. The Lucky Lettuce Company has reaction coefficients of 1.1 for the first factor and 0.4 for the second. The expected return is therefore
a. 0.087.
b. 0.147.
c. 0.190.
d. 1.500.

4.10 In the Roll-Ross model, the only factor which does not involve unanticipated changes is
a. the default-risk premium.
b. industrial production.
c. the term structure of interest rates.
d. expected inflation.

ANSWERS

4.1	a	p.	88	4.6	c	p.	92
4.2	b	pp.	88-89	4.7	c	p.	93
4.3	a	p.	90	4.8	c	pp.	93-94
4.4	d	p.	91	4.9	b	p.	96
4.5	b	p.	92	4.10	d	p.	97

CHAPTER 5

VALUATION FROM A RELATIVE STANDPOINT

PERSPECTIVE

A call option gives the holder the right to buy a share of stock at a specified price until the expiration date. The value of the option depends on the price volatility of the stock, the length of time to expiration, and the prevailing interest rate.

Hedging involves taking opposite positions in a stock and its option to eliminate risk. The value of a hedged position does not change when the stock price changes. In efficient financial markets, the rate of return on a perfectly hedged position would be the risk-free rate.

The Black-Scholes option pricing model provides an exact formula for determining the value of an option based on the volatility of the stock, the price of the stock, the exercise price of the option, the time to expiration of the option, and the short-term interest rate.

Options are also available on stock indices, foreign currencies, debt instruments, and futures contracts.

CHAPTER OUTLINE

I. Options are contracts that give the holder the right, but not the obligation, to buy (call option) or sell (put option) a designated security at a specific price for a limited time.
   A. A European option can be exercised only at its expiration date; an American option can be exercised at any time up to and including the expiration date.
   B. The profit or loss on a call option is calculated as:
      1. the value of the option at the expiration date less the price, or "premium," paid for it by the investor.
      2. the premium received by the writer (the seller) less the value of the option at the expiration date.
   C. The value of a European call option at its expiration date is the larger of either:
      1. the stock price at expiration less the exercise price; or
      2. zero.
   D. The current market value, or premium, of a call lies between two boundaries.
      1. Its maximum value is the market price of the stock.
      2. Its minimum value is the current stock price less the exercise price, or zero, whichever is greater.

E. The premium paid for a call option, within its boundaries, depends upon several factors.
   1. The farther away the expiration date, the higher the premium.
   2. The higher the interest rate applied in calculating the present value of the exercise price to be paid in the future, the higher the premium.
   3. The greater the price volatility of the underlying stock, that is, the greater the possibility of a big increase in the stock's price, the higher the premium.
   4. The lower the exercise price, the higher the premium.
   5. The higher the current stock price, the higher the premium.

II. Hedging involves taking opposite positions in a stock and its option to eliminate risk. Price movements in one security will be offset by opposite price movements in the other.
   A. For an investor who buys stock and writes calls, the appropriate
      Hedge Ratio = $(uV_0 - dV_0)/(uV_s - dV_s)$, where
      V_s = current market price of stock,
      uV_s = price of stock at expiration: V_s times one plus a percentage increase,
      dV_s = price of stock at expiration: V_s times one minus the percentage,
      V_0 = current premium on option,
      uV_0 = value of option corresponding to uV_s,
      dV_0 = value of option corresponding to dV_s.
   B. For example, suppose a $20 stock is expected to change 10 percent during the next six months. A call option with an exercise price of $19 is written now. To calculate the appropriate hedge ratio, we need to first calculate:
      uV_s = ($20)(1.10) = $22,
      uV_0 = $22 - $19 = $3,
      dV_s = ($20)(0.90) = $18,
      uV_0 = 0 because $18 - $19 < 0.
      Hedge Ratio = ($3 - 0)/($22 - $18) = 3/4.
      The investor who wishes to hedge should purchase three shares of stock and write four call options.
   C. Whichever direction the stock takes, the hedge will be worth $54 at expiration:
      (3)($22) - (4)($3) = $54
      (3)($18) - (4)(0) = $54
   D. In an efficient market, the call premium will adjust until the return on the hedged position is the risk-free rate. Suppose for our transaction above, the risk-free rate is 5 percent for six months. The premium on the call can be determined by solving the following equation for V_0:
      $(3V_s - 4V_0)(1.05)$ = $54
      $($60 - 4V_0)(1.05)$ = $54
      $4.2V_0$ = $9
      V_0 = $2.14

28

III. The Black-Scholes option model can be used to determine the equilibrium value of an option.
  A. It is based on a number of assumptions, some of which can be relaxed.
    1. Only European options are considered.
    2. There are no transaction costs.
    3. Options and stocks are infinitely divisible.
    4. Information is available to all without cost.
    5. No imperfections exist in writing an option or selling a stock short.
    6. The short-term interest rate is known and constant throughout the duration of the option contract. Market participants can both borrow and lend at this rate.
    7. The stock pays no dividend.
    8. Stock prices behave in a manner consistent with a random walk in continuous time.
    9. The probability distribution of stock returns over an instant of time is normal.
    10. The variance of the return is constant over the life of the option contract.
  B. It allows an investor to establish a riskless hedged position, but that position must be continually adjusted as time passes and as the stock price changes.
  C. The equation for the Black-Scholes model is:
    $V_0 = V_s N(d_1) - (E/e^{rt}) N(d_2)$, where
    V_0 = the current value of the option,
    V_s = the current price of the stock,
    E   = the exercise price of the option,
    e   = 2.71828
    r   = the short-term annual interest rate, continuously compounded,
    t   = the length of time in years to the expiration of the option,
    $N(d)$ = the value of the cumulative normal density function,
    d_1 = $[\ln(V_s/E) + (r + \sigma^2/2)t]/\sigma t^{1/2}$
    d_2 = $[\ln(V_s/E) + (r - \sigma^2/2)t]/\sigma t^{1/2}$
    ln   = the natural logarithm
    σ = the standard deviation of the annual rate of return on the stock continuously compounded.
  D. The hedge ratio is $N(d_1)$. If it were 0.5, the investor would purchase one share of stock for every two options written.
  E. In solving the Black-Scholes equation, the stock price, exercise price time of expiration, and short-term interest rate are known; the standard deviation of the stock price must be estimated from recent history and extrapolated to the near future.
  F. Some of the assumptions of the model can be relaxed.
    1. Transactions costs and delays in execution preclude continuous adjustment to maintain a risk-free hedge. In

a stable market, adjustments may be made once or twice a week.
2. American and European options on non- dividend-paying stocks will be priced the same if they are alike in all other respects.
3. American options on dividend-paying stocks require that the Black-Scholes model be modified. But these modifications have a tendency to overestimate option values for "in the money" options and options written on high-variance stocks. They also tend to underestimate option values for "out of the money" options and options written on low-variance stocks.

IV. In addition to stock options, there are options on other securities.
   A. An index option is written on a broad portfolio of stocks.
   B. A foreign currency option is written on a specific number of units of a major foreign currency.
   C. Debt options are written on specific debt instruments, such as Treasury bills, notes, and bonds.
   D. Interest rate options are written on futures contracts which promise delivery of specific debt instruments such as Eurodollars or Treasury securities.
      1. If interest rates rise and security prices fall, the buyer of the futures contract, the call option holder, and the put option writer lose, while the writer of the futures contract, the call option writer, and the put option holder gain.
      2. If interest rates fall and security prices rise, all the above gain and loss positions are reversed.
   E. Financial institutions making fixed-rate loan commitments face one-sided risk: rising interest rates. They are therefore purchasers of interest rate puts or writers of interest rate calls.
   F. Valuation models for debt options are modifications of the Black-Scholes model.

APPENDIX.
   In the equilibration process driven by arbitrage, put, call, and stock prices are precisely related. The put-call parity theorem can be expressed as:
   either $V_C - V_P = V_S - PV(E)$
   or $V_C - V_P - V_S + PV(E) = 0$, where
      V_C = value of call option,
      V_P = value of put option,
      V_S = value of a share of stock,
      $PV(E)$ = present value of exercise price.
The interest rate used to calculate present value is the short-term rate for the time to expiration of the options. This theorem may be used to determine whether the stock and the options are priced correctly.

MULTIPLE CHOICE QUESTIONS

5.1 European options and American options differ because
   a. with American options the holder receives any cash dividends paid.
   b. with European options the holder receives any cash dividends paid.
   c. European options can be exercised only at the expiration date.
   d. American options can be exercised only at the expiration date.

5.2 The value of a call option at the expiration date is
   a. the maximum of the exercise price less the value of the stock, and zero.
   b. the maximum of the stock price less the exercise price, and zero.
   c. the exercise price.
   d. the stock price.

5.3 For a call option that has time before the expiration date, the price should be
   a. greater than the theoretical value of the option.
   b. exactly equal to the theoretical value of the option.
   c. less than the theoretical value of the option.
   d. equal to the price of the stock.

5.4 When the stock price is greater than the exercise price, the call option is said to be
   a. ahead of the money.
   b. in the money.
   c. at the money.
   d. out of the money.

5.5 Which of the following is generally the most important factor in determining the value of an option with significant time remaining before expiration?
   a. the volatility of the stock price
   b. the risk-free rate
   c. the length of the option
   d. the expected rate of return on the stock

5.6 Which of the following is not a factor in determining the value of a call option?
   a. the risk-free rate
   b. the current price of the stock
   c. the volatility of the stock return
   d. the expected rate of return on the stock

5.7   In order to set up a hedge we
      a. buy stock and buy calls.
      b. sell stock and sell calls.
      c. buy stock and sell calls.
      d. buy Treasury bills and sell calls.

5.8   The hedge ratio is the number of
      a. shares of stock purchased for each call written.
      b. calls written for each share of stock sold.
      c. puts written for each share of stock purchased.
      d. shares of stock purchased for each call purchased.

5.9   The value of the option is determined by a strategy which is
      expected to
      a. maximize the expected return on the hedged position.
      b. generate a risk-free return on the hedged position.
      c. maximize the expected return on the stock.
      d. break even.

5.10 In the Black-Scholes Option Model, the hedge ratio is
      a. $N(d_1)$.
      b. $N(d_2)$.
      c. e^{rt}.
      d. $\ln(V_s/E)$.

ANSWERS

5.1	c	pp.	105-106		5.6	d	p.	111
5.2	b	p.	106		5.7	c	p.	112
5.3	a	pp.	107-108		5.8	a	p.	112
5.4	b	p.	109		5.9	b	pp.	113-114
5.5	a	p.	109		5.10	a	p.	116

CHAPTER 6

PRINCIPLES OF CAPITAL INVESTMENT

PERSPECTIVE

Capital budgeting refers to the internal long-term investment decisions of a firm which involve an outlay of current funds to obtain future cash inflows. The numbers needed for analysis are incremental cash flows.

The capital budgeting methods considered are the average rate of return, payback, internal rate of return, and net present value. This last method is judged superior for several reasons.

Suboptimal decisions can be made if careful attention is not given to capital rationing restrictions and to the biases caused by anticipated inflation.

The acquisition of all or part of another company can be treated as a capital budgeting problem.

CHAPTER OUTLINE

I. When making a capital investment, a company decides to incur a current cash outlay for benefits to be received in the future.
   A. The expected return on this investment must meet or exceed the return required by investors.
   B. Successful administration of capital investments by a company involves:
      1. generation of investment proposals,
      2. estimation of cash flows for the proposals,
      3. evaluation of these cash flows,
      4. selection of projects based on an acceptance criterion,
      5. continual reevaluation of investment projects after their acceptance.
   C. For each investment proposal, information must be provided on expected incremental cash flows on an after-tax basis.
      1. Initial cash outflows include purchase and installation of new equipment, less cash obtained from scrap on the trade-in of old equipment, plus additional marketing, personnel, or other required expenditures.
      2. Cash inflows include incremental after-tax sales revenues.
      3. Subsequent cash outflows include incremental labor and maintenance costs, material costs, and various other tax-deductible expenses.

33

4. Sunk costs must be ignored.
5. Appropriate opportunity costs must be considered.
6. Interest costs are embodied in the required rate of return and should not be double-counted in the cash outflows.
7. Depreciation is not included because it is a noncash expense, but the tax saving on incremental depreciation charges is a cash inflow.
8. The after-tax salvage value of the project must also be considered.

D. In evaluating a group of investment proposals, their independence, or lack of it, must be considered.
1. Two or more proposals are mutually exclusive if the acceptance of one precludes acceptance of the other(s).
2. A contingent or dependent proposal requires the acceptance of one or more other proposals.

II. The following methods can be used to evaluate investment proposals.
A. The average rate of return represents the ratio of the average annual profits after taxes to the investment in the project. Its principal advantage is its simplicity. It has two disadvantages.
1. It is based on accounting income instead of on cash flows.
2. It ignores the time value of money.
B. The payback period calculates the number of years required to recover the initial cash investment. It functions better as a risk-averting constraint than as a profit-maximizing measure. It has two disadvantages.
1. It ignores all cash flows after the payback period.
2. It ignores the timing of cash flows within the payback period.
C. The internal rate of return (IRR) is the discount rate that equates the present value of the expected cash outflows with the present value of the expected cash inflows.
1. If the IRR meets or exceeds a required rate of return, the project is accepted; if not, it is rejected.
2. Different types of investment projects may require different rates of return.
D. The net present value method (NPV) discounts all cash flows to their present value, using the required rate of return.
1. If the sum of these discounted cash flows is zero or more, the project is accepted; if not, it is rejected.
2. Alternatively expressed, the project will be accepted if the present value of cash inflows exceeds the present value of cash outflows.
E. The profitability index (PI), or benefit-cost ratio, of a project is the present value of the future net cash flows divided by the initial cash outlay.
1. If the profitability index is 1.0 or larger, the project is accepted; if not, it is rejected.

2. The PI recognizes that the initial cash outflow is discretionary; subsequent cash outflows are not. It is more rational than the aggregate index (AI), which is the present value of cash inflows divided by the present value of cash outflows.

III. The three discounted cash flow methods are comparable but not equal.
   A. In evaluating a single project, NPV, IRR, and PI give the same accept-reject signals.
   B. In choosing between mutually exclusive projects, NPV is preferred to PI because it expresses the expected economic contribution of the project in absolute, rather than relative, terms.
   C. In choosing between mutually exclusive projects, NPV and IRR may give conflicting results.
      1. The IRR method implies that funds are compounding at the internal rate of return; the NPV method implies that funds are compounding at the required rate of return.
      2. The IRR ignores the scale of the project, while the NPV expresses results in absolute terms.
      3. If the cash-flow stream changes sign more than once, multiple internal rates of return may result.
   D. Although many managers may feel more comfortable using IRR when comparing projects, the NPV method always provides correct rankings of mutually exclusive investment projects.
   E. It is possible to construct a NPV profile, which is a graph portraying the relationship between the NPV of a project (on the Y-axis) and the discount rate employed (on the X-axis).
      1. At the Y-intercept, where the discount rate is zero percent, NPV equals total cash inflows less total cash outflows.
      2. As the discount rate increases, the NPV for a conventional project decreases.
      3. The profile crosses the X-axis at the IRR, the point where NPV equals zero.
      4. If the profile crosses the X-axis more than once, the cash flow stream is unconventional and has multiple rates of return.

IV. The 1986 Tax Reform Act establishes eight property classes for depreciation purposes. (See Table G at the back of this book.)
   A. For the 3-, 5-, 7-, and 10-year property classes, the method of depreciation is the 200 percent declining-balance method.
      1. The taxpayer is allowed to switch to straight line depreciation in the year that provides the quickest write-off.
      2. A half-year convention is used in the first year and in the year following the last year.

B. For the 15- and 20-year property classes, 150 percent declining-balance depreciation is used, with subsequent switching to straight line.

C. For the 27 1/2- and 31 1/2-year property classes, straight-line depreciation is used throughout.

V. In calculating periodic net cash flows, many things must be taken into consideration.

A. The annual net cash flows are on an after-tax basis and are calculated as:

$A_i = C_i(1-t) + D_i(t)$, where

A_i = annual net cash flow in period i,

C_i = incremental cash inflows less outflows,

t = corporate tax rate,

D_i = annual depreciation charge in period i.

B. At the end of the project, the after-tax salvage value must be included in A_i.

C. Investment in a fixed asset sometimes requires an investment in working capital--the carrying of additional cash, receivables, and/or inventories.

1. This supplementary investment is treated as a cash outflow when incurred, usually in time period 0.

2. It is presumed returned at the end of the project, resulting in a cash inflow in time period n.

VI. Economic factors may result in distorted capital budgeting decisions.

A. Capital rationing occurs anytime there is a budget ceiling, or constraint, on the amount of funds that can be invested during a specific period of time.

1. The financial manager must select the combination of investment proposals that provides the highest total NPV, subject to the budget constraint.

2. Proposals that have positive NPVs may have to be rejected, which is suboptimal investment policy.

3. Capital rationing for more than one period requires that the financial manager also consider the net cash inflows provided by the projects in their early years; these cash inflows will ease subsequent budget constraints.

B. Inflation causes a decline in real after-tax cash flows because depreciation charges do not change in keeping with inflation. Taxes therefore increase at a rate faster than inflation.

C. Inflation bias arises in capital budgeting when the discount rate contains an element of capital cost attributable to inflation expected by the market, but the cash flows expected by the company ignore inflation. Potential investments are thereby underappraised.

VII. The acquisition of all or part of another company can be treated like a capital budgeting problem.

A. The buying company should first estimate the after-tax future cash income that the acquisition is expected to bring in.
   1. Synergy, the concept that "2 plus 2" can produce 5, must be considered.
   2. Expected revenues less expected costs and the capital expenditures necessary to sustain, and hopefully improve, the expected revenues constitute "free cash flows."
   3. Because the after-acquisition capital structure may be modified, interest charges should not be considered in the calculation of cash flows.
   4. Any new investments the acquiring firm believes it will have to make in order to generate the expected stream of earnings must be considered.
   5. Acquisition analysts usually assume a 20-year cash flow horizon even though the post-acquisition company has an infinite life.
B. Estimation problems arise because, in most cases, the price to be paid for the acquisition is not set and must be negotiated.
   1. Payment to the acquired company's stockholders may involve common stock, preferred stock, debt, cash, or some combination.
   2. If securities other than cash are used in the acquisition, they should be converted to their cash-equivalent market values.
   3. If the acquiring firm assumes the liabilities of the acquiree, these should be converted to their cash-equivalent market values.
   4. The present value of future incremental free cash flows represents the maximum cash-equivalent price to be paid.

APPENDIX:
   The occurrence of multiple rates of return depends upon the number of reversals of sign and the magnitude of cash flows.
   1. A nonconventional investment has more than one reversal in sign; therefore, solving for the IRR produces more than one root.
   2. The number of roots equals the number of sign reversals, but some of the roots may be imaginary numbers (multiples of the square root of -1.0).
   3. When real multiple roots exist, none is a measure of investment worth.
The best way to evaluate a nonconventional investment is the NPV method.

MULTIPLE CHOICE QUESTIONS

6.1 Most firms screen proposals at multiple levels of authority.
    How high a proposal must go before it is finally approved
    usually depends on its
    a. length of time.
    b. risk.
    c. size.
    d. number of times being considered.

6.2 If we are considering buying a new machine to replace an old
    one, the net cash flow in the first year includes
    a. depreciation on the new machine.
    b. the tax saving on the depreciation on the new machine.
    c. the change in depreciation from the old machine to the new.
    d. the tax saving on the change in depreciation.

6.3 The average rate of return is calculated by dividing
    a. average income by the present value of the cash inflows.
    b. the present value of the inflows by the initial cost.
    c. average income by the initial cost.
    d. the present value of the inflows by the present value of
       the outflows.

6.4 Which of the following methods is least desirable for
    evaluating capital investments?
    a. internal rate of return
    b. net present value
    c. profitability index
    d. payback

6.5 Capital investment decisions should be made on the basis of
    the present value of the
    a. incremental cash flows.
    b. sunk costs.
    c. total cash flows.
    d. salvage value.

6.6 If the acceptance of one project precludes the acceptance of
    another project, the projects are said to be
    a. redundant.
    b. mutually exclusive.
    c. dependent.
    d. contingent.

6.7 If the net present value of an investment is negative,
    a. the IRR will be negative.
    b. the profitability index will be less than zero.
    c. the profitability index will be less than one.
    d. the IRR will be zero.

6.8 When the discount rate used is increased, NPV
     a. falls.
     b. rises.
     c. stays the same.
     d. may rise or fall.

6.9 The implicit reinvestment rate assumed in using the IRR method
     is
     a. the risk-free rate.
     b. the internal rate of return.
     c. the external rate of return.
     d. the required rate of return.

6.10 Working capital related cash flows are
     a. inflows.
     b. outflows.
     c. both inflows and outflows.
     d. of no consequence in capital budgeting.

ANSWERS

6.1 c p. 135   6.6 b p. 143
6.2 d p. 138   6.7 c pp. 144-145
6.3 c p. 140   6.8 a p. 146
6.4 d p. 140   6.9 b p. 147
6.5 a p. 143   6.10 c p. 151

CHAPTER 7

RISK AND MANAGERIAL OPTIONS
IN CAPITAL BUDGETING

PERSPECTIVE

Both the expected profitability and the risk of investment proposals must be analyzed. Risk is the standard deviation of possible net present values or possible internal rates of return.

Risk can be measured under the assumption of serial independence or dependence of cash flows over time. Decision trees, simulation techniques, and the portfolio approach are all useful in analyzing risky investments.

Management may have the option, or flexibility, to alter a previous investment decision by expansion, abandonment, or postponement. These options can affect the desirability of a capital budgeting project. In analyzing managerial options, decision trees are often used.

CHAPTER OUTLINE

I. It is necessary to measure the overall riskiness of an investment proposal when the probability distributions of cash-flow outcomes for different periods are not necessarily the same.
  A. If cash flows are independent from period to period, the outcome in period t does not depend on the outcome in period t-1.
    1. The NPV for a project is calculated as:

    $$NPV = \sum_{t=0}^{n} \overline{A}_t / (1 + i)^t, \text{ where}$$

      $\overline{A}_t$ = mean net cash flow in period t,
      i = risk-free rate,
      n = number of periods over which cash flows are expected.
    2. The standard deviation of possible cash flows for a single period, t, is calculated as

    $$\sigma_t = [\sum_{x=1}^{m} (A_{xt} - A_t)^2 P_{xt}]^{1/2}, \text{ where}$$

      A_{xt} = xth possible net cash flow,
      m = number of possible net cash flows,
      P_{xt} = probability of occurrence of A_{xt}.

3. The standard deviation of the probability distribution of net present values is then

$$\sigma = [\sum_{t=0}^{n} \sigma_t^2/(1 + i)^{2t}]^{1/2}.$$

4. If the probability distribution of NPVs is approximately normal, one can calculate the probability that a proposal will provide a NPV of less or more than a specified amount. One needs to determine the area under the curve to the left or right of a particular point of interest. Thus,

   $S = (X - NPV)/\sigma$, where

   S = number of σs X is away from the mean,

   X = point we are interested in, usually 0.

   Table F (at the back of the book) for S, which will give the area in the tail of the distribution.

5. $S < 0$ indicates the left tail; $S > 0$, the right tail.

B. One can create a probability distribution of possible internal rates of return by varying the discount rate, i, in (3) above, to obtain standard deviations for each variation. Then one can calculate the probability that NPV < 0 for each σ.

C. The main difficulty associated with risky investments lies in obtaining the cash-flow estimates, not in the subsequent mathematical manipulation of the data.

1. If the incentive compensation of managers is linked to the return on assets relative to their expected return, managers are likely to submit estimates which are biased downward.

2. An individual may make unbiased cash-flow estimates for projects in his area, but management may tend to select those projects whose costs are underestimated and revenues overestimated.

3. As a proposal rises through the chain of command, adjustments for bias may be made and overadjustment may result.

4. Because capital investment projects involve returns over many years, it is difficult to evaluate biases by comparing forecasts with actual results.

D. Cash flows are perfectly correlated over time if actual cash flows for all periods show the same relative deviation from the means of their respective probability distributions.

1. The expected NPV and σ_t are calculated exactly the same as in the case of independence.

2. The equation for the standard deviation of the probability distribution of NPVs becomes

$$\sigma = \sum_{t=0}^{n} \sigma_t/(1 + i)^t.$$

3. The probability that NPV will be less or more than a specified amount remains the same as in the case of independence.

E. When the cash flows for a project are neither approximately independent nor perfectly correlated over time, the project can be evaluated by using a series of conditional probability distributions.
   1. For a simple project, the calculation of expected NPV and σ_t are unchanged, and the standard deviation can be calculated as

   $$\sigma = [\sum_{x=1}^{L} (NPV_x - \overline{NPV})^2 P_x]^{1/2}, \text{ where}$$

   NPV_x = NPV for series x of net cash flows for periods 0 to n,
   $\overline{NPV}$ = expected or mean NPV of proposal,
   L = number of series,
   P_x = probability of occurrence of the xth series.
   2. For a complex project, one can approximate σ by means of simulation. Random sampling is used to select cash-flow series for evaluation and $\overline{NPV}$ or $\overline{IRR}$ and σ are estimated from the sample.

II. When multiple investment projects are involved, risk measurement may differ from that for a single project because of diversification.
   A. A "portfolio" of capital assets differs from a portfolio of securities.
      1. Capital assets usually are not divisible; securities are.
      2. It is usually expensive, and sometimes impossible, to sell off a capital asset; securities are usually marketable.
      3. Securities do not involve problems of mutual exclusion and contingency; assets do.
   B. The mean NPV for the combination is a weighted average of the NPVs of the individual component projects.
   C. The standard deviation of the probability distribution of possible NPVs for a portfolio of capital investments can be calculated as

   $$\sigma = (\sum_{j=1}^{m} \sum_{k=1}^{m} r_{jk}\sigma_j\sigma_k)^{1/2}, \text{ where}$$

   m = total number of assets in the portfolio,
   r_{jk} = expected correlation between the NPVs for investments j and k,
   σ_j = standard deviation for investment j,
   σ_k = standard deviation for investment k.
   D. The higher the degree of positive correlation, and/or the greater the standard deviations of the individual projects, the greater the standard deviation of the portfolio of the projects.
   E. Projects in the same general line of business tend to be highly correlated with each other, while projects in

essentially unrelated lines of business tend to have low degrees of correlation.

    F. It is possible to analyze feasible combinations of existing projects and proposals under consideration, according to their NPVs and σs, to see which combinations dominate. The dominant combinations correspond to the efficient frontier for an opportunity set of security portfolios.

III. After investment projects are accepted, managers often can make changes which affect subsequent cash flows and/or the life of the project.

    A. The types of managerial options available include:

        1. the option to vary output depending on conditions. A variant on this is the option to distribute a new product either regionally or nationally. This option is best valued by use of a decision tree.

        2. the option to abandon a project

            a. when its abandonment value exceeds the present value of the project's subsequent future cash flows and

            b. when its future abandonment values will be lower. This option is best valued by use of conditional probabilities.

        3. the option to postpone a project. By waiting, management trades off the interim cash flows for new information.

    B. The presence of managerial options enhances the worth of an investment project.

        1. Project worth = NPV + Option value.

        2. The greater the number of options and the greater the uncertainty surrounding their use, the higher the option value.

        3. Managerial options are much more difficult to value than financial options because:

            a. one cannot use risk neutrality to factor out implied variances,

            b. the exercise price of a managerial option can change over time,

            c. volatility is difficult to measure,

            d. the opportunity cost of waiting to exercise a managerial option is not precise.

        4. Recognition of management flexibility can alter an initial decision to accept or reject a project.

MULTIPLE CHOICE QUESTIONS

7.1 Whether cash flows are dependent, independent, or partially correlated over time affects the calculation of
   a. expected net present value.
   b. expected internal rate of return.
   c. the standard deviation of possible cash flows for a period.
   d. the standard deviation of net present value.

7.2 Unbiased cash flow forecasts
   a. can be obtained by linking management's compensation to the ratio of achieved versus expected return on assets.
   b. cannot be obtained if only one individual is responsible for making cash flow forecasts.
   c. can be obtained by using decision tree approaches to adjust for bias.
   d. can be obtained by careful selection of projects.

7.3 For cash flows which are correlated over time, the σ of NPVs will be _____ the σ of NPVs for cash flows which are independent over time.
   a. larger than
   b. equal to
   c. smaller than
   d. half of

7.4 Moderate correlation between cash flows over time
   a. is best ignored.
   b. can be dealt with by using conditional probability distributions.
   c. never happens.
   d. requires the use of the calculus.

7.5 Simulation models
   a. rely on variations on two factors.
   b. assume many random combinations of variables.
   c. produce good results with a minimum number of trials.
   d. will not work if the factors are independent of each other.

7.6 Diversification of capital assets is similar to diversification of securities
   a. because capital assets are not divisible.
   b. because it is easy to sell off capital assets.
   c. in the measurement of risk.
   d. if there are no contingency problems.

7.7 Capital projects may be highly correlated to each other
   a. in the same general line of business.
   b. in essentially unrelated lines of business.
   c. only for manufacturing companies.
   d. almost never.

7.8   A combination of investment projects
    a. dominates a second combination when the second's NPV is the same and its σ is higher than the first's.
    b. contains only new projects.
    c. is only feasible if its NPV > 0 and σ = 0.
    d. is acceptable if it is not on the efficient frontier.

7.9   Managerial options
    a. are marketable.
    b. are the equivalent of financial options.
    c. decrease the worth of a project.
    d. increase the worth of a project.

7.10 An investment project should be abandoned when
    a. it can be sold for more than book value.
    b. its abandonment value exceeds the present value of its subsequent future cash outflows.
    c. put options on the company's stock are available.
    d. the depreciation schedule is switched from declining-balance to straight-line.

ANSWERS

7.1	d	p.	171		7.6	c	p.	180
7.2	c	p.	174		7.7	a	p.	181
7.3	a	pp.	175-176		7.8	a	pp.	182-183
7.4	b	p.	176		7.9	d	p.	184
7.5	b	pp.	178-179		7.10	b	p.	189

CHAPTER 8

CREATING VALUE THROUGH CAPITAL INVESTMENTS

███

PERSPECTIVE

In seeking capital investments with excess returns in order to increase shareholder wealth, a company can evaluate risky investments by using a market model such as CAPM or APT factor.

To use the model, investment project returns can be expressed in terms of changes in calculated value. A publicly traded proxy company can be used in place of the market portfolio, and beta can be adjusted for mismatched leverage.

Project evaluation with the adjusted present value (APV) method discounts operating cash flows at the unlevered cost of equity and interest tax shields at the cost of borrowing, then deducts flotation costs from the sum of the two present values.

Instead of using a market model, one can evaluate projects with respect to their incremental impact on the total return and risk of the firm. When we allow for bankruptcy costs and other market imperfections, residual risk becomes important. Instead of reconciling the two approaches, a dual system of evaluating risky investments is recommended.

CHAPTER OUTLINE

I. Corporations in an attractive industry and/or which attain a sustainable competitive advantage within an industry can earn returns exceeding the return required by the financial markets for the risk involved.
   A. Attractive industry characteristics include:
      1. the growth phase of a product cycle,
      2. barriers to entry,
      3. protective devices such as patents, temporary monopoly power, and/or oligopoly pricing.
   B. Competitive advantage involves the relative position of a company within an industry, and can be eroded by competition.

II. The investor's required rate of return is the return on a risk-free asset plus the market price of risk that cannot be avoided by diversification.
   A. If the security market line (SML) of the CAPM were the appropriate equilibrium tradeoff between risk and required return, then all projects with expected IRRs above the SML

should be accepted, resulting in an increase in share price.

B. If both the product markets and the capital markets were perfect, there would be no excess returns (points above the SML).

C. Because a project's systematic risk is the same for all firms, its required rate of return is the same for all firms. But its expected return can vary among firms because of differences in expertise and efficiency.

D. If information is available about the actual returns on individual assets, investors can effectively diversify across capital assets of individual companies. Investment projects should therefore be evaluated on the basis of only their systematic risk, not on the basis of their total risk or the incremental risk they contribute to the firm.

III. The required rate of return for a project can be expressed as a function of its beta, in a CAPM context, or of its factor risks, in an APT factor model context.

A. To calculate the required rate of return, it is necessary to make some initial assumptions.

1. The project is financed entirely by equity.

2. The firm considering the project is financed entirely by equity.

3. All financial market information pertains to unlevered situations.

B. The profitability of an investment project has to be restated as a one-period return.
$R_t = (V_t + A_t - V_{t-1})/V_{t-1}$, where
V_t = market value of the project at the end of period t,
A_t = net cash flow received at the end of period t.

C. A project may be similar to a company whose stock is publicly traded.

1. That company's beta can be used as a proxy for the project's beta in a CAPM context.

2. That company's responsiveness coefficients can be used as a proxy for the project's responsiveness coefficients in an APT factor model context.

D. If a proxy publicly traded company is not available, but we assume that rates of return in the future will be like those in the past, we can collect historical data and estimate beta for the project by running the regression
$Y_t = a + bX_t + e_t$, where
Y_t = historical one-period return on a comparable project in year t,
X_t = excess return of a market index (annual return on the S&P 500 Index less annual yield on short-term Treasury securities),
a = estimate of intercept,
b = estimate of beta, or β_k,
e_t = annual estimation errors.

E. The required rate of return for the project can be estimated as
$$R_k = R_f + (\bar{R}_m - R_f)\beta_k, \text{ where}$$
   R_k = required rate of return for the project,
   R_f = risk-free rate,
   $\bar{R}_m$ = arithmetic mean of S&P 500 Index returns,
   β_k = beta for the project.
F. R_k can then be used to discount the future cash flows of the project to calculate its NPV.

IV. Beta is a function of both business risk and leverage; it is important that the beta used for the project corresponds with the way the firm intends to finance.
A. When the leverage of the proxy company differs significantly from the leverage the firm wishes to employ, the beta of the proxy company should be adjusted.
B. Because interest payments are deductible for tax purposes, the required rate of return for a stock is
$$R_j = R_f + [(\bar{R}_m - R_f)/\sigma_m^2](r_{ju,m}\sigma_{ju}\sigma_m)[1 + (D/S)(1-T_c)] \text{ where,}$$
   σ_m = standard deviation of the probability distribution of possible market returns,
   σ_{ju} = standard deviation of the probability distribution of possible returns for security j in the absence of leverage,
   $r_{ju,m}$ = correlation coefficient between returns for security j in the absence of leverage and the market portfolio,
   T_c = corporate tax rate,
   D/S = debt-to-equity ratio in market value terms.
C. β_{ju} is the beta measuring the responsiveness of the excess return for the security in the absence of leverage to the excess return for the market portfolio, and
$$\beta_{ju} = r_{ju,m}\sigma_{ju}\sigma_m/\sigma_m^2.$$
D. The required rate of return for a stock can be restated as
$$R_j = R_f + (\bar{R}_m - R_f)\beta_{ju}[1 + (D/S)(1-T_c)], \text{ where}$$
   $(\bar{R}_m - R_f)\beta_{ju}$ = premium for business risk,
   $(\bar{R}_m - R_f)\beta_{ju}(D/S)(1-T_c)$ = premium for financial risk.
E. The observed beta for a stock, β_j, embodies both risks, so that
$$\beta_j = \beta_{ju}[1 + (D/S)(1-T_c)].$$
F. Therefore, the beta for a stock in the absence of leverage is
$$\beta_{ju} = \beta_j/[1 + (D/S)(1-T_c)].$$
G. Given these expressions, one can derive the beta in the absence of leverage for a particular stock, and then adjust it for the degree of leverage one wishes to employ.
   1. Suppose the beta for the proxy company is 1.20, its debt ratio is 1/3, and its tax rate is 40 percent. Beta in the absence of leverage would be calculated as
   $$\beta_{ju} = 1.20/[1 + (1/3)(1 - .4)] = 1.00.$$

2. Now suppose one employs a debt ratio of 0.5, and a tax rate of 30 percent. The adjusted beta is then calculated as
$$\beta_j = (1.00)[1 + (.5)(1 - .3)] = 1.35.$$

H. This beta adjustment procedure assumes that capital markets are perfect except for the presence of corporate taxes.
  1. If future debt levels and the tax shield are uncertain, the unlevered beta will be less than estimated and the required rate of return will be overestimated.
  2. If the debt issued is risky, the unlevered beta will be higher than estimated and the required rate of return will be underestimated.

V. Once calculated, the adjusted beta is used to determine the cost of equity capital for the project. The required return for the project is the weighted average cost of capital.
  A. The cost of debt (R_D) is calculated on an after-tax basis.
  B. the cost of equity (R_E) is calculated, using the adjusted beta, as
$$R_E = R_f + (\overline{R}_m - R_f)B_j.$$
  C. The weighted average cost of capital (WACC) is expressed as
  WACC = $W_D R_D + W_E R_E$, where
    W_D = proportion of debt,
    W_E = proportion of equity,
    $W_D + W_E = 1.0$.
  D. This WACC is the discount rate to be used when calculating NPV.
  E. This procedure assumes that a project's beta is approximately constant over time. If it is not, there are various adjustment techniques.
    1. It may be appropriate to use different betas and therefore different discount rates for different future periods.
    2. The certainty-equivalent technique would derive cash-flow betas instead of return betas and use them to reduce the expected cash flows for systematic risk.

VI. The adjusted present value method (APV) is an alternative to the WACC approach. It breaks down cash flows into two components: unlevered operating cash flows and cash flows associated with financing the project.
  A. The formula for the adjusted present value is
$$APV = \sum_{t=0}^{n} OC_t/(1+k_u)^t + \sum_{t=0}^{n} (I_t)(T_c)/(1+k_i)^t - F, \text{ where,}$$
    OC_t = after-tax operating cash flow in period t,
    k_u = required rate of return in absence of leverage,
    I_t = interest payment on debt in period t,
    T_c = corporate tax rate,
    k_i = cost of debt financing,
    F = after-tax flotation cost associated with financing (debt, equity, or both).

B. If a company should depart radically from previous financing patterns and/or invest in an entirely new line of business, then the APV approach gives a more accurate portrayal of the project's worth than the WACC approach.
C. For most situations, APV and WACC give identical accept/reject decisions.

VII. If the critical assumptions of CAPM and the APT factor model do not hold, management should consider the marginal impact of an investment proposal on the risk complexion of the firm as a whole. Unsystematic risk may affect the value of the firm.
A. In this case, the portfolio approach should be considered.
   1. The expected value and standard deviation of the probability distribution of possible NPVs for all feasible combinations of existing projects and investment proposals under consideration must be calculated.
   2. Management's utility preferences with respect to NPV and σ will determine the selection of the most desirable combination of investments.
B. When insolvency or bankruptcy costs are significant, investors require that management consider the total risk of the firm, not just systematic risk.
C. There are other market imperfections which minimize the investors' ability to diversify away unsystematic risk.
   1. The borrowing rate typically exceeds the lending rate.
   2. There are transactions costs.
   3. Investors incur costs in obtaining information.
D. It is recommended that management consider the impact of a project on both the systematic risk and the total risk of the firm. If one approach gives an accept signal and the other a reject signal, whichever approach is more applicable to the specific company should prevail.

MULTIPLE CHOICE QUESTIONS

8.1 When using the CAPM in a capital budgeting context, which of the following is not true?
   a. Beta is assumed to be constant during the project.
   b. Determination of beta is more difficult than with securities.
   c. Acceptance of projects which fall above the SML should result in a decrease in the stock price.
   d. If product markets were perfect, all projects should fall on the SML.

8.2 Theoretically, the same project will be more valuable to some firms than others because of all the following except
   a. management efficiency.
   b. synergy.
   c. differences in cash flows.
   d. the required return.

8.3 According to the CAPM, diversification by a firm in its portfolio of capital assets is
a. beneficial if the returns are not correlated.
b. beneficial if the returns are correlated.
c. not beneficial.
d. worth accepting a lower rate of return.

8.4 When using a proxy company's beta as an estimate of the project beta, the object is to come up with a beta that
a. portrays the business risk of the project.
b. portrays the interest rate risk of the project.
c. will vary with the life of the project.
d. will approximate the average market beta.

8.5 Which piece of information is not needed in order to use the CAPM to determine the required rate of return on a risky project?
a. the risk-free rate
b. the standard deviation
c. the expected market return
d. the project beta

8.6 Given a project's systematic risk, the acceptance rate should be
a. greater for the firm with more debt.
b. less for the firm with more debt.
c. the same for only those firms with no debt.
d. the same for all firms.

8.7 Assume that you have determined the beta for a proxy company in order to estimate beta for a particular project. The unadjusted proxy beta will be larger than the project beta due to
a. debt in your firm.
b. debt in the proxy firm.
c. market imperfections.
d. rounding.

8.8 Assume the cost of debt is 12 percent, the tax rate is 40 percent, the risk-free rate is 10 percent, the expected market return is 15 percent, and the project beta (adjusted for the debt-equity ratio of 2/3) is 1.2. The required average return is approximately
a. 10.1 percent.
b. 12.5 percent.
c. 14.4 percent.
d. 16.0 percent.

8.9 The adjustment of betas for leverage and the APV both attribute the effects of leverage to be because of
   a. bankruptcy costs.
   b. transactions costs.
   c. tax shields.
   d. discounting.

8.10 The probability of a firm becoming insolvent is a function of a firm's
   a. systematic risk.
   b. nonsystematic risk.
   c. residual risk.
   d. total risk.

ANSWERS

8.1 c p.   205
8.2 d p.   207
8.3 c p.   208
8.4 a pp. 208-209
8.5 b p.   214
8.6 b p.   214
8.7 b p.   217
8.8 a pp. 217-218 $R_D = (12\%)(1 - .4) = 7.2\%$
                      $R_E = 10\% + (15\% - 10\%)(1.2) = 16\%$
                      $WACC = (2/3)(7.2\%) + (1/3)(16\%) = 10.1\%$

8.9 c p.   219
8.10 d p.   222

███

CHAPTER 9

PERSPECTIVE

If a company's activities and investment proposals are homogeneous with respect to risk, the market-value weighted average cost of capital can be computed and used as an acceptance criterion.

Measurement of the costs of debt and preferred stock are fairly straightforward, but there is more than one way to calculate the cost of equity.

The condition of homogeneity may be met for divisions of the company but not for the company as a whole. The proxy company approach can be used to find a leverage-adjusted required rate of return for divisions. Adjustments for unsystematic risk can also be included.

When evaluating acquisitions, diversification is not a thing of value. Only synergism generates excess returns. Under certain conditions, the diversification effect might be important in mergers, and equity holders and debt holders might expropriate wealth from each other.

CHAPTER OUTLINE

I. The use of an aggregate required rate of return is appropriate only when a company's assets and proposed investments are homogeneous with respect to risk.
   A. The weighted average cost of capital is composed of the costs of the various components of financing and may be used as the aggregate required rate of return.
      1. The cost of equity capital may be defined as the required return on a security and obtained from the CAPM or APT factor equations.
         a. It is the investor's before-tax return but the company's after-tax cost.
         b. It assumes financial markets are highly efficient.
         c. It assumes bankruptcy costs are negligible.
         d. It must be adjusted (usually upward) for real-world market imperfections.
      2. Alternatively, the cost of equity capital may be defined as the market rate of discount that equates the present value of all expected future dividends per share with the current market price of the stock.

  a. It applies to all dividend-growth situations.

  b. It serves as a benchmark for adjusting the required rate of return.

 3. The cost of debt is the discount rate that equates the net proceeds of the debt issue with the present value of interest plus principal payments after taxes.

  a. Individual debt instruments are replaced over time, but debt is never really paid off.

  b. The company is assumed profitable enough to utilize the tax shield on interest paid.

  c. The corporate tax rate is assumed to be constant.

 4. The cost of preferred stock is the stated annual dividend divided by the proceeds of the stock issue. It is not adjusted for taxes.

  a. Tax law provides that 70 percent of the dividends received by a corporation are exempt from taxation.

  b. Dividends are payable at the discretion of the board of directors.

B. Because market values are used in the calculation of the costs of the various financing components, market-value weights should be used.

C. Because the firm raises capital marginally to make a marginal investment in new projects, the weights employed must be marginal. If these do not match the existing capital structure, an obvious bias results.

 1. In practice, a firm may finance with debt in one instance and with equity in another. These are temporary deviations.

 2. Over time, most firms are able to finance in roughly a proportional manner.

 3. If a firm wishes to change its capital structure, the target weights should be used.

D. Flotation costs reduce the amount of funds a company receives from the sale of new securities. There are two ways to handle this.

 1. The flotation costs of financing can be added to the project's initial cash outlay, thereby reducing the NPV.

 2. The discount rate can be adjusted upward when flotation costs are present, producing an "adapted" cost of capital. It has been shown that this produces a biased estimate of NPV.

E. Accepting projects yielding more than the weighted average required return will increase the market price of the common stock.

 1. If the equity-financed portion of the new investment project consists of a common stock offering, dividends per share must rise to overcome the dilution effect.

 2. If the equity-financed portion of the new investment project consists of retained earnings, no dilution occurs but the present value of the incremental dividends must exceed the equity capital employed.

3. If investment projects are financed out of a pool of funds, most of the benefit of the excess return will accrue to the stockholders because the maximum claims of debt and preferred stockholders are fixed.

F. For a multiproduct firm with investment proposals of varying risk, the use of an overall required rate of return (the WACC) is inappropriate.

G. If a project lowers the relative risk of the firm because of diversification properties, it may enhance debt holder wealth at the expense of stockholders. According to the text, the project should be rejected by management even though it has a positive NPV to security holders overall.

II. Where the use of a companywide cost of capital is inappropriate, the use of a divisional cost of capital may be valid.

A. The CAPM can be used to determine a required rate of return on equity for a division by finding proxy companies that are engaged solely in the same line of business as the division.

B. The amount of nonequity financing assigned to a division should approximate the same relative amount as that used by the company. If the proportions are not nearly the same, the proxy company's beta should be adjusted before it is used.

C. The company's overall borrowing cost is used as the cost of debt for a division, but adjustments can and should be made if a division has significantly more or less risk than the company as a whole.

D. If a company allocates the same proportion of nonequity funds to each of its divisions, the weighting process and the calculation of the weighted average required rate of return are the same as for the whole company.

E. If different divisions are allocated significantly different proportions of nonequity funds, the company may have problems.

1. High leverage for one division may cause the cost of debt for the overall company to rise.

2. High leverage for one division may increase the uncertainty of the tax shield associated with debt for the company as a whole.

3. High leverage for one division increases the volatility of returns to stockholders of the company, and increases the possibility of insolvency and bankruptcy costs being incurred. In turn, this raises the company's required return on equity.

F. Alternatively, the WACC of the division can be approximated by determining the WACC of proxy companies.

III. Capital should be allocated or transferred throughout the firm on a risk-adjusted return basis.

A. The higher the systematic risk of a division, the higher the required return should be.
B. If a single cutoff rate is used for project selection in a multidivision firm, the company may become riskier without commensurate increases in expected return.
   1. Projects whose expected returns are below the company's WACC but above the division's WACC will be rejected.
   2. Projects whose expected returns are above the company's WACC but below the division's WACC will be accepted.
C. Thus a company may pour money into those divisions providing the greatest growth opportunities and risk, and ration capital to "safe" divisions.
D. If imperfections in the capital markets make the unsystematic risk of a firm significant to investors, a dual approach for evaluating risky investments should be used.
   1. Investment proposals should be evaluated according to a market model and accept/reject decisions made.
   2. Investment proposals should also be evaluated according to their incremental impact on the total risk of the firm and accept/reject decisions made.
   3. When conflicting decisions are reached, the final decision depends on the perceived importance of imperfections in the capital markets.

IV. Given the assumptions of a market model, acquisition for diversification alone will not enhance shareholder wealth.
   A. The purchase price of a prospective acquisition is the market value of its debt plus the amount paid to the stockholders of the acquired company.
   B. The expected incremental after-tax cash flows arising from the acquisition, discounted at the weighted average required return for the acquired company, must exceed the purchase price.
   C. The present value of cash flows will exceed the purchase price only if the acquisition will lead to operating economies and/or improved management.
   D. Lacking synergies, the market price of the acquirer's stock will fall below the level it would have been if the acquisition had not been made.
   E. If imperfections in the market exist and unsystematic risk is important, then an acquisition can be treated as one more investment proposal in a portfolio of projects to be considered.
   F. Other things constant, mergers can result in "financial synergism."
      1. The debt capacity of the postmerger company will be greater than the sum of the capacities of the original two companies because the relative dispersion of cash flows will have been reduced.

2. If debt is cheaper than equity because of the tax shield, borrowing more will increase the value of the equity.
G. Under perfect capital market assumptions, however, borrowing more will not change the total value of the firm.
1. The market price of the debt rises and the market price of the equity falls.
2. Wealth is transferred from stockholders to bondholders.
H. By diversifying through a merger, the probability of bankruptcy can be reduced. If the costs of bankruptcy were positive and significant before the acquisition, then this reduction will increase the value of the firm.
I. If a merger permits the losses of one firm to be applied against the profits of the other, future taxes paid may be less for the merged company than for the two firms separately. This reduction will increase the value of the merged firm.

MULTIPLE CHOICE QUESTIONS

9.1 The use of a companywide cost of capital is appropriate when the projects
a. are homogeneous with respect to return.
b. are homogeneous with respect to risk.
c. have net present values near zero.
d. have little risk.

9.2 The cost of equity is the
a. rate required by stockholders.
b. rate that makes the NPV zero.
c. rate on the market portfolio.
d. same as the firm's cost of capital.

9.3 The discount rate that makes the present value of the expected dividend stream equal to the market price of the firm's stock is
a. the cost of debt.
b. the cost of equity.
c. the cost of capital.
d. the return on the market portfolio.

9.4 When the dividends are expected to grow perpetually at a constant rate, the required rate of return can be estimated by
a. $D_1/P_1 + g$.
b. $D_0/P_0 + g$.
c. $D_1/P_0 + g$.
d. $D_0/P_1 + g$.

9.5   Debt is the least costly component because of
       a. low risk.
       b. corporate taxes.
       c. both low risk and corporate taxes.
       d. its small proportion of the capital structure.

9.6   The appropriate weights to use in determining the weighted
       average cost of capital are
       a. marginal and book value weights.
       b. marginal and market value weights.
       c. historical and book value weights.
       d. historical and market value weights.

9.7   Flotation costs should be
       a. ignored.
       b. considered in calculating the component costs.
       c. considered in calculating the cash flows.
       d. considered in determining the weights.

9.8   If a proxy company for a division must be chosen to use the
       CAPM in calculating the division's required return on equity,
       that proxy should have all of the following except
       a. nearly the same degree of unsystematic risk.
       b. nearly the same degree of systematic risk.
       c. similar products and services.
       d. approximately the same proportion of nonequity financing.

9.9   If a multi-divisional firm were to use one WACC for evaluating
       all investment proposals, over time the firm would
       a. become more conservative.
       b. accept more projects from its lower risk divisions.
       c. become more risky.
       d. accept fewer projects from its more risky divisions.

9.10   If the assumptions of the CAPM hold, the most important reason
       for mergers is
       a. diversification.
       b. reduction in taxes.
       c. synergy.
       d. increased debt capacity.

ANSWERS

9.1 b p.   235   9.6   b pp. 241-242
9.2 a p.   235   9.7   c p.   243
9.3 b p.   237   9.8   a p.   248
9.4 c p.   238   9.9   c p.   250
9.5 c pp. 239-240   9.10 c p.   253

CHAPTER 10

THEORY OF CAPITAL STRUCTURE

████████████████████████████████████

PERSPECTIVE

One of the decisions confronting financial managers is the acquisition of funds for investment. The objective is to acquire funds at the lowest possible cost so as to maximize the market price of the firm's stock. The decision thus requires an analysis of whether or not the source of funds affects the price of funds. Put differently, is there an optimal capital structure for the firm?

In a perfect market environment capital structure was found not to matter. The presence of market imperfections, incentives, and financial signaling leads to the conclusion that firms indeed do have an optimal capital structure.

CHAPTER OUTLINE

I. The issue of whether or not capital structure affects the firm's total valuation is generally approached by ignoring all factors except leverage.
   A. Development of a model requires an extensive array of assumptions:
      1. no corporate or personal income taxes, and no bankruptcy costs,
      2. a change in capital structure is effected immediately,
      3. no transaction costs,
      4. all earnings are passed on to shareholders as dividends,
      5. all investors view market profitability similarly,
      6. firms are operating in a no growth environment.
   B. The effect of a changing degree of leverage is analyzed using
      $k_o = k_i [B/(B + S)] + k_e [S/(B + S)]$, where,
      k_o = the weighted average cost of capital = O/V,
      k_i = yield on corporate debt = F/B,
      k_e = required return on equity = E/S,
      B = market value of debt outstanding,
      S = market value of stock outstanding,
      O = net operating earnings,
      V = total market value of the firm,
      F = annual interest charges,
      E = earnings available to common stockholders,
      B/S = degree of leverage.

C. The net operating income approach implies that the total valuation of the firm and share price are unaffected by the financial structure and, thus, there is no optimal structure.
   1. Assumes that k_o is constant regardless of the degree of leverage.
   2. The cost of debt funds remains the same regardless of the degree of leverage.
   3. The required return on equity increases linearly with leverage.
   4. The reduction in the cost of capital arising from an increase in the use of "cheaper" debt funds is exactly offset by an increase in the required equity return.
D. The traditional approach assumes that there is an optimal capital structure.
   1. At lower levels of debt the increase in k_e does not offset the benefits of using lower costing debt financing.
   2. At higher levels of debt the increase in k_e, due to greater risk, more than offsets the benefits of debt financing.

II. Modigliani and Miller (MM) originally stated that there is no optimal capital structure.
   A. This conclusion was based on a very limiting set of assumptions:
      1. capital markets are perfect and information is costless,
      2. expected future earnings are the same as present operating earnings,
      3. firms can be categorized by risk class,
      4. no corporate income taxes.
   B. The total investment value of a corporation depends on its underlying profitability and risk, not on the financial mix.
   C. Arbitrage is the leveling force postulated by MM.
      1. Investors could substitute personal borrowing for corporate leverage.
      2. If an equal risk, higher return opportunity were available, investors would flock to it and thus equilibrate the returns.
   D. Equilibrium occurs across securities of different companies on the basis of total expected value and risk, as demonstrated by the CAPM.
      1. The systematic risk of the overall firm is the weighted average of the betas of the individual securities of the firm.
      2. An increase in the debt-to-equity ratio increases both the expected return of a stock and its beta.
      3. Perfect markets cause proportionate increases, thereby canceling out the effect on share price.

III. The presence of income taxes creates imperfections in the capital markets, which may affect the firm's valuation and cost of capital.
  A. Interest payments are a deductible business expense.
    1. The total income to all investors is larger for leveraged firms.
    2. Assuming debt to be employed permanently, the present value of the tax shield is
       PV of tax shield = $[(t_c)(r)(B)]/r = t_cB$, where
         t_c = corporate tax rate,
         r = interest rate on debt,
         B = market value of the debt.
    3. The greater the amount of debt, the greater the tax shield and the greater the value of the firm.
    4. The MM proposition, adjusted for corporate taxes, requires a strategy of maximum leverage.
    5. However, the modified MM proposition is not consistent with corporate behavior.
  B. The value of the tax shield is uncertain.
    1. It is earnings dependent.
    2. Tax laws may change.
    3. The presence of alternative tax shelters produces tax shelter redundancy.
  C. The presence of personal income taxes may reduce or eliminate the corporate tax advantage associated with debt.
    1. Equal personal tax rates on the returns on debt and on stock retains the corporate tax advantage.
    2. The effective tax on capital gains, due for example to its postponability, is less than that on interest and dividend income, even with identical federal tax rates.
    3. If the company is concerned with the after-tax income to the investors, its financing decisions would depend on the relative value of the corporate and personal tax rates.
      a. If the personal tax rate on debt income exceeds the corporate tax rate, then debt financing is preferable.
      b. Otherwise, stock financing is preferable.
  D. Miller advocated that personal and corporate tax effects cancel out, thus, capital structure is irrelevant.
    1. He assumes that the personal tax rate on stock income is zero and that the personal tax rate on debt income equals the corporate tax rate.
    2. When there is unsatisfied demand for debt more will be issued. This process will continue until the marginal tax rate of the debt clientele equals the corporate tax rate. At this point the market for debt and stock is in equilibrium and the individual company cannot increase its total value by changing the amount of debt in its capital structure.
    3. A number of issues have been raised relative to Miller's argument:

a. the acceptance of a zero personal tax on stock income is suspect;

b. since 1986, the highest tax bracket for personal income is less than that for corporate taxes;

c. based on the relationship between yields on corporate bonds and on tax-exempt bonds, there appears to be only a 25 percent personal tax rate on debt.

4. It appears that in reality the tax advantage associated with leverage is reduced but not eliminated; the optimal capital structure should contain a large amount of debt.

IV. Bankruptcy costs produce market imperfections which affect capital structure decisions.

A. To the extent that a leveraged firm has a greater possibility of bankruptcy than a unleveraged firm, it is a less attractive investment.

B. The possibility of bankruptcy increases at an increasing rate as the debt-to-equity ratio increases.

C. Although the creditors bear the ex post costs of bankruptcy, the stockholders bear the ex ante costs and the subsequent lower valuation of the firm.

D. Recent studies have shown that the costs of bankruptcy will differ according to the type of firm.

E. The combined effect of taxes and bankruptcy costs produce a tradeoff which results in there being an optimal capital structure for the firm.

V. Several additional imperfections are present in the capital markets.

A. Personal and corporate leverage may not be perfect substitutes.

B. Restrictions on institutional investment behavior may retard the arbitration process.

VI. Incentive issues and agency cost can influence the choice of security used in financing.

A. Owning stock can be viewed as owning a call option.

1. The writer of the option is the debt holder.

2. The exercise price is the face value of the debt: the expiration date is the maturity of the debt.

3. If the value of the firm is greater than the face value of the debt, the stockholders will exercise their option and pay off the debt.

4. If the value of the firm is less than the debt, the option will not be exercised. The bondholders get all available value and the stockholders receive nothing.

B. The greater the variance in value of the underlying asset, the greater the value of the option.

1. It is in the interest of the stockholder to increase the variance of the firm.

2. Increasing the proportion of debt in the capital structure increases variability and, thus, the value of the stock.
C. Debt holders should protect themselves by imposing restrictive covenants on the firm at the time of debt issuance.
D. New investments, even those with negative NPV, which increase risk substantially, could be acceptable to stockholders if there is a sufficient wealth transfer from debt holders to stockholders accompanying the increased risk.
E. Since stockholders have incentives to take actions contrary to the interests of the debt holders, the actions of the stockholders need to be monitored.
1. Monitoring involves agency costs which ultimately are borne by stockholders.
2. Debt holders could get their protection in the form of higher interest rates rather than through restrictive covenants.
3. As debt becomes a larger proportion of the capital structure, the increasing monitoring costs act as a disincentive to the issuance of more debt.
F. It may be that a high debt ratio creates incentives for management to increase efficiency in order to survive.

VII. Financial signaling is based on the concept of asymmetric information, that is, management has better information about the firm than do stockholders.
A. Management should always finance an investment project by issuing the overvalued security.
B. The issuance of debt is thus considered "good news" as it implies that the existing stock is undervalued.
C. Capital structure changes do not necessarily cause changes in valuation; it is the signal conveyed by the change that affects valuation.

MULTIPLE CHOICE QUESTIONS

10.1 The optimal capital structure is the combination of debt and equity which
   a. maximizes the value of the debt.
   b. maximizes the value of the equity.
   c. maximizes the value of the firm.
   d. maximizes the firm's cost of capital.

10.2 The traditional approach regarding capital structure suggests that as leverage increases, the cost of capital
   a. increases and then decreases.
   b. decreases and then increases.
   c. is constant.
   d. increases at a decreasing rate.

10.3 The net operating income approach suggests that in the absence of income taxes, as leverage increases, the value of the firm
a. increases and then decreases.
b. decreases and then increases.
c. is constant.
d. increases at a decreasing rate.

10.4 Assume that Firms A and B are exactly alike except that Firm A has more debt than Firm B. Further assume that the price of Firm A's stock is higher than the price of Firm B's stock. Finally assume the Modigliani-Miller assumptions with no taxes. Modigliani-Miller suggest that the arbitrager will
a. sell Firm A stock, borrow and buy Firm B stock.
b. sell Firm B stock, borrow and buy Firm A stock.
c. sell Firm A stock, lend and buy Firm B stock.
d. sell Firm B stock, lend and buy Firm A stock.

10.5 Assume that B is the market value of debt, r is the interest rate on the debt and T_c is the corporate tax rate. If the tax shield were certain, the value of the tax shield would be
a. rB.
b. rT_c.
c. $T_c B$.
d. $rT_c B$.

10.6 As leverage increases, the net value of the uncertain tax shield would
a. increase at a constant rate.
b. increase at an increasing rate.
c. increase at a decreasing rate.
d. remain constant.

10.7 When personal taxes are considered, the value of the tax shield is
a. increased if the tax rate on debt income equals the tax rate on stock income.
b. decreased if the tax rate on debt income equals the tax rate on stock income.
c. decreased if the tax rate on debt income is greater than the tax rate on stock income.
d. increased if the tax rate on debt income is greater than the tax rate on stock income.

10.8 Which of the following tends to increase the amount of debt in the capital structure?
a. corporate taxes
b. personal taxes
c. bankruptcy costs
d. institutional restrictions

10.9 Assume a firm increases the proportion of debt in the capital structure by issuing new debt which is not subordinate to any existing debt. Option theory suggests that
a. existing stockholders lose because their risk increases.
b. existing debt holders lose and stockholders gain.
c. new debt holders gain and old debt holders lose.
d. both old debt holders and stockholders gain.

10.10 Monitoring costs, providing complete protection,
a. tend to increase the debt in the capital structure.
b. are always paid by debt holders.
c. are always borne by equity holders.
d. increase the operational efficiency of the firm.

ANSWERS

10.1	c	p.	268	10.6	c	p.	278
10.2	b	pp.	270-271	10.7	c	pp.	279-280
10.3	c	p.	270	10.8	a	p.	286
10.4	a	pp.	272-273	10.9	b	p.	289
10.5	c	p.	277	10.10	c	p.	293

CHAPTER 11

MAKING CAPITAL STRUCTURE DECISIONS

PERSPECTIVE

There are a number of methods of analysis that can be brought to bear on the determination of an appropriate degree of leverage for a company. These methods include EBIT-EPS analysis, an examination of the company's cash-flow ability to service debt, a comparison of the company's leverage ratio relative to others, surveying investment analysts and lenders, and evaluating the effect of a financing decision on the company's securities ratings. The implicit cost of leverage is its effect on a stock's value in the marketplace.

CHAPTER OUTLINE

I. The financial manager must determine an approximate proportion of debt to employ to maximize share price.
   A. Comparing alternative methods of financing is one way to analyze the relationship between earnings before interest and taxes (EBIT) and earnings per share (EPS).
      1. A break-even or indifference chart can be constructed, with EBIT on the X-axis and EPS on the Y-axis.
      2. EPS is defined as:
         $[(EBIT - C_i)(1 - t) - D_{pi}]/S_i$, where
         C_i = interest for the ith financing alternative,
         t = corporate tax rate,
         D_{pi} = dividend on preferred stock for the ith financing alternative,
         S_i = number of shares of common stock for the ith financing alternative.
      3. For each financing alternative, a straight line shows EPS for all levels of EBIT ≥ 0.
      4. An indifference point, where the lines cross, is the point where there is no difference in EPS between the two financing alternatives.
      5. For levels of EBIT lower than the indifference point between debt and common stock, the common stock will provide the higher EPS.
      6. For levels of EBIT higher than the indifference point between debt and common stock, the debt is the better financing alternative.
      7. There is no indifference point between debt and preferred stock; the debt is always better.

8. The indifference point between any two financing alternatives can be found mathematically by solving the following equation for EBIT:
$$[(EBIT - C_1)(1 - t) - D_{P1}]/S_1 =$$
$$[(EBIT - C_2)(1 - t) - D_{P2}]/S_2$$
If the equation has no solution, the lines do not intersect.
B. An EBIT-EPS chart does not permit a precise analysis of risk, but certain generalizations are possible.
1. The greater the level of EBIT and the lower the probability of downside fluctuation, the stronger the case for the use of debt.
2. A probability distribution of possible levels of EBIT can be superimposed on the EBIT-EPS chart.
3. Use of more than one method of analysis of leverage gives better insight into the return-risk tradeoff.

II. Several methods of evaluating the risk associated with increased leverage are available.
A. The use of coverage ratios increases our knowledge about the debt capacity of the firm.
1. A times interest earned ratio of exactly 1:1 indicates that earnings are exactly sufficient to satisfy the current interest burden, and is a cause for concern. A ratio much less than 3:1 may only be appropriate for a highly stable set of circumstances. The ratio is defined as:
$$\text{Times interest earned} = \frac{EBIT}{\text{Interest on debt}}.$$
2. A debt-service coverage ratio recognizes that the inability to meet a principal payment constitutes the same legal default as failure to meet an interest payment. Because principal payments are made out of after-tax earnings, they must be adjusted so that they are consistent with EBIT. The ratio is defined as:
$$\text{Debt-service coverage} = \frac{EBIT}{(\text{Interest} + \text{Principal})/(1-t)}.$$
3. A debt-service coverage ratio (DSCR) of 1.20 means that EBIT can fall by only 16.67 percent before earnings coverage is insufficent to service the debt. The calculation is as follows:
$$\text{Decline in EBIT} = 1 - (1/\text{DSCR})$$
$$= 1 - (1/1.20) = 0.1667$$
4. While lease financing and preferred stock dividends are not debt per se, their impact on cash flows is exactly the same as the payment of interest and principal on a debt obligation. Annual lease payments should therefore be added to the numerator and annual lease payments and dividends should be added to the denominator in the debt-service coverage ratio to get a fixed-charges coverage ratio.
B. Two comparisons should be undertaken with a coverage ratio.

67

1. It should be compared with past and expected future ratios of the same company to detect any improvement or deterioration over time; this is called trend analysis.
2. It should be compared with the same ratio for similar companies.
C. Some analysts use EBITD, adding depreciation back to EBIT, to portray the actual cash flow of a company. Because some capital expenditures are necessary to keep the business operating and may be approximated by depreciation, EBITD is not a good measure of the cash available for debt service.

III. The chances of cash insolvency are not adequately measured by coverage ratios; some measure of the possible deviation of actual cash flows from those expected is needed.
A. Cash budgets can be prepared for a range of possible outcomes, with a probability attached to each.
1. Cash budgets consider more than expected earnings: the purchase or sale of assets, the liquidity of the firm, dividends, seasonal patterns, and any other factors impacting on cash flows.
2. Given the probabilities of particular cash-flow sequences, the financial manager can determine the amount of fixed charges and debt the company can undertake without violating management's insolvency limits.
3. A similar approach examines the cash flows of the company under the most adverse circumstances to determine whether cash balances will be involuntarily reduced below zero. Probabilities can be included in this analysis, if desired.
B. Cash inadequacy is said to occur if the firm is out of cash after making certain desired expenditures such as dividends, R&D expenditures, and capital expenditures.
1. Cash insolvency is the extreme form of cash inadequacy.
2. An inventory of the company's resources available to meet an unexpected cash drain should be developed. Ranging from the least to the most serious alternative, they are as follows:
   a. Contingency reserves can be tapped in a short period of time. They include: surplus cash, unused lines of credit, additional bank loans, additional long-term debt, and new equity.
   b. Changes in operations produce cash over time and usually affect long-term profitability adversely. They include reductions in: the volume of production, marketing expenditures, R&D expenditures, administrative overhead, capital expenditures, and dividend payments.
   c. The most drastic source of cash is the liquidation of assets.

3. Once an inventory of resources has been compiled, the adequacy of these resources should be judged in relation to potential cash drains.
C. Sophisticated lenders and institutional investors analyze the amount of fixed charges and the ability of the firm to service these charges, but individual investors may judge financial risk by the book value ratio of debt to equity.
   1. Companies in the same industry may have similar business risk and would, therefore, be expected to have approximately the same capital structure.
   2. A firm whose capital structure is significantly different from comparable companies' structures should be prepared to justify its position.

IV. To evaluate the impact of a financial decision on share price, the financial manager must consider evaluations of the company being done "outside."
   A. Institutional investors and investment analysts analyze many companies and have relevant views on the appropriate amount of leverage.
   B. Lenders have definite limits on how much debt can be undertaken before the cost of borrowing starts to rise.
   C. Management may develop a "feel" from what has happened to the market price of the stock when the company issued debt in the past.
   D. Whenever a company sells a debt or preferred stock issue to public investors instead of privately, it must have the issue rated by one or more rating services.
      1. The principal rating agencies are Moody's Investors Service and Standard and Poor's.
      2. Both agencies use a system of letter grading in an attempt to rank issues according to their probability of default.
      3. The first four grades are considered investment-quality issues; the remaining five grades are considered speculative and such issues are ineligible for investment by many insitutional investors.
      4. While the assignment of a rating for a new issue is current, changes in ratings of existing securities tend to lag the events that prompt the change.
      5. A significant lowering of a security rating usuallly is a manifestation of fundamental problems that may raise the implicit as well as the explicit cost of leverage.

V. Once a company has determined an appropriate capital structure, it still has the problem of timing security issues.
   A. Frequently, a company must decide whether to finance now with a stock issue and later with a debt issue, or vice versa.
   B. If the future were certain, the optimal financing sequence for many years to come could be determined by taking

advantage of known future changes in the stock and fixed-income securities markets.
    C. When a firm issues debt, the financial signal given usually raises the stock price, but the firm sacrifices a certain amount of flexibility.
    D. A company cannot issue debt continually without building its equity base, which is why flexibility is important.
    E. To preserve its flexibility in tapping the capital markets, it may be better for a company to issue stock now and save its unused debt capacity for future needs.

APPENDIX:
    A. Bankruptcy costs reduce the optimal degree of leverage and take two forms.
        1. Direct bankruptcy costs involve fees and other compensation to third parties and represent a direct cash drain from suppliers of capital.
        2. Indirect costs are represented by the decrease in value arising from the delays and economic inefficiencies of operating a company which is about to go bankrupt.
        3. Studies suggest that indirect costs are larger than direct costs.
    B. The doctrine of absolute priority calls for the claims of one class of claimants to be settled in full before there is any distribution to a junior claimant.
        1. Stockholder-oriented management has bargaining power, because it controls the company during reorganization proceedings and may protract the proceedings and incur costs borne largely by creditors.
        2. Creditors may give up part of their claim to expedite the process.
        3. This "willing" shifting away of wealth from creditors has the effect of reducing bankruptcy costs overall.

MULTIPLE CHOICE QUESTIONS

11.1 The optimal capital structure can be
    a. determined precisely by EBIT-EPS analysis.
    b. determined precisely by use of coverage ratios.
    c. determined precisely by cash budgeting.
    d. only estimated within some range.

11.2 XYZ Company has $1,000,000 of 10 percent debt, $200,000 of 12 percent preferred stock, and 100,000 shares of common stock outstanding. It is subject to a tax rate of 40 percent. If its expected EBIT is $1,000,000, what is its expected EPS?
    a. $5.25
    b. $5.16
    c. $4.76
    d. $4.16

11.3 An existing firm will expand its assets by $1,000,000. It
has three plans to raise the funds. Plan 1 involves issuing
common stock, Plan 2 will use debt, and Plan 3 will use
preferred stock. Regardless of the EBIT, the EPS for Plan 2
will always be
a. less than the EPS for Plan 1.
b. more than the EPS for Plan 1.
c. less than the EPS for Plan 3.
d. more than the EPS for Plan 3.

11.4 Firm ABC is currently an all-equity firm with 1 million
shares of common stock outstanding. It is considering
expanding and will choose between two alternative plans for
raising the needed cash. Plan 1 is to issue $1,000,000 in 10
percent debt. Plan 2 is to issue 500,000 new shares of
common stock at $2 per share. The firm is subject to income
taxes at the rate of 40 percent. What level of EBIT will
result in the same EPS for the two plans?
a. zero
b. $300,000
c. $600,000
d. $900,000

11.5 The appropriate times interest earned value is
a. zero or better.
b. one or better.
c. three or better.
d. a function of the business risk of the firm.

11.6 Suppose a company has $1,500,000 of 10 percent debt with a
$150,000 principal payment. It also has $1,000,000 of 10
percent preferred stock and 100,000 shares of common stock
outstanding. It is subject to a 40 percent tax rate. If its
EBIT is $600,000, what is its times interest earned?
a. 4.00
b. 2.00
c. 1.50
d. 1.06

11.7 In the short term, the key in being able to meet debt
payments is
a. revenue.
b. to lower expenses.
c. earnings.
d. cash.

11.8 If a firm anticipates a condition known as "cash inadequacy,"
the resources available to meet a cash drain the fastest are
a. obtaining additional bank loans.
b. changing the production schedule.
c. reducing administrative overhead.
d. liquidating assets.

71

11.9 A security with which of the following ratings would be eligible for investment by all institutional investors?
a. A-3
b. Ba-1
c. B-2
d. CCC

11.10 In order to keep the cost of capital low and to be flexible from a financing standpoint, a company should maintain a capital structure
a. of all debt.
b. of all equity.
c. within the target range but at the low end of the debt level.
d. within the target range but at the high end of the debt level.

ANSWERS

11.1 d p. 305

11.2 b p. 306 $\dfrac{(\$1,000,000 - 100,000)(0.6) - \$24,000}{100,000} = \$5.16$

11.3 d p. 307

11.4 b p. 307 $\dfrac{(EBIT - \$100,000)(0.6)}{1,000,000} = \dfrac{0.6EBIT}{1,500,000}$

$15(EBIT - \$100,000) = 10 \ EBIT$

$EBIT = \$300,000$

11.5 d p. 309

11.6 a p. 309 $\$600,000/(\$1,500,000)(0.10) = 4.00$

11.7 d pp. 311-312

11.8 a pp. 312-313

11.9 a p. 315

11.10 c p. 317

CHAPTER 12

DIVIDEND PAYOUT RATIO AND VALUATION

PERSPECTIVE

If dividends affect the value of common stock, dividend policy is more than a passive variable determined solely by the investment opportunities available to a company.

With perfect capital markets and an absence of taxes, dividend payout is irrelevant. Some market imperfections favor increased retention, others favor increased payout. Differential taxes on dividends and capital gains, flotation costs, and the existence of various types of stockholders favor retention. Restrictions on financial institutions, investor psychology, and financial signaling favor dividend payout.

Because many companies behave as if dividend policy is relevant, there are many factors management must consider when faced with a dividend decision.

CHAPTER OUTLINE

I. Each period the firm must decide whether to retain its earnings or to distribute part or all of them to shareholders as cash dividends.
   A. The residual theory of dividend policy implies that dividends are irrelevant; the investor is indifferent between dividends and retention by the firm.
      1. If investment opportunities promise a return greater than the required return, investors want the company to retain its earnings.
      2. If the expected return on opportunities is less than the required return, investors prefer dividends.
      3. A firm may smooth out actual payments by saving some funds in surplus years, in anticipation of deficit years.
   B. Modigliani and Miller argue that dividends are irrelevant because the effect of dividend payments on shareholder wealth is offset exactly by other means of financing.
      1. A stock's decline in market price because of external financing offsets exactly the payment of the dividend.
      2. The total amount of financing by the sale of new stock is determined by the amount of investments in a period which cannot be financed by retained earnings.

3. Shareholder wealth is unaffected by current and future dividend decisions; it depends entirely on the expected future earnings stream of the company.
4. If leverage is also irrelevant, then it makes no difference whether investment opportunities are financed with debt, common stock, or retained earnings.
5. In a world of perfect capital markets and no taxation, investors can manufacture "homemade" dividends, which are perfect substitutes for corporate dividends, by selling shares if dividends are less than desired or purchasing additional shares if dividends are more than desired.
C. The existence of market imperfections can make dividends relevant.
1. Corporate income taxes have no bearing on dividend relevance because dividends are not a tax-deductible expense.
2. For many investors, there exists a present-value differential in personal taxes between a dollar of dividends and a dollar of retained earnings.
   a. The investor clientele neutrality theory argues that if various clienteles of investors have dividend preferences, corporations will adjust their dividend payout to take advantage of this situation and the result is an equilibrium point where no company can affect its share price by altering its dividend.
   b. Theoretically, investors can use combinations of put and call options to isolate movements in stock price, effectively stripping the dividend from the capital gains component of the stock.
   c. Another tax avoidance strategy suggests borrowing to the extent that interest payments offset dividends received, neutralizing the risk of borrowing by purchasing an insurance annuity, and postponing the realization of capital gains.
3. For each dollar paid out in dividends, a company nets less than a dollar after flotation costs per dollar of external financing.
   a. The smaller the size of the issue, the greater the flotation costs as a percentage of the total amount of funds raised.
   b. Small issues are difficult to sell even with high flotation costs.
4. Stockholders who desire more (or less) current income must pay brokerage fees on the sale (or purchase) of shares of their stock.
   a. These fees vary inversely (per dollar of stock sold) with the size of the sale.
   b. The smallest marketable integer is one share, which may not meet income needs exactly.
5. Restrictions on institutional investors can influence the desirability of dividends.

a. If a company does not pay a dividend or has not paid dividends for some time, certain institutional investors are not permitted to invest in the stock.
b. Universities have restrictions on the expenditure of capital gains from their endowment and a number of trusts have a prohibition against the liquidation of principal.
6. For psychological reasons, some investors prefer dividends.
a. To the extent that dividends provide information on economic earnings not provided by reported accounting earnings and other sources, share price will respond to a change in the payout ratio.
b. It is generally agreed that the signaling effect is more important for dividends than it is for capital structure.

II. Empirical testing of dividends' impact on valuation has taken several forms.
A. Stock prices decline on the ex-dividend day, but by less than the amount of the dividend, because of the tax advantage of capital gain income relative to dividend income.
B. Studies of the relationship between dividend yields and stock returns have had mixed results.
1. A modified CAPM approach to measure the deviation of a stock's dividend yield from that of the market portfolio found that dividend policy does not matter.
2. Many studies have found that high-dividend stocks provide higher expected before-tax returns than low-dividend stocks, to offset the tax effect.
3. When a default-risk premium variable is added to an extended CAPM, the dividend coefficient loses its significance, suggesting that it is likely to be correlated with a number of economic phenomena.
4. After the passage of the 1986 Tax Reform Act, dividend payout ratios of American corporations increased somewhat, which is consistent with the lessening of the differential taxation between dividends and capital gains.
C. There have been two major types of studies for a financial signaling effect.
1. Event studies of daily share price changes, relative to the market, have shown that increases in dividends lead to positive excess returns and decreases to negative excess returns.
2. A study of firms initiating dividends for the first time or after a long hiatus found significant excess returns, indicating that dividends convey valuable information to investors over and above that available from other sources.

III. There are a number of factors that firms can and should analyze when establishing or changing a dividend policy.
   A. Cash budgets and projected source and use of funds statements can be used to determine the likely cash flows and cash position of the company, and to evaluate if anything is left over after servicing its funds needs, including profitable investment projects. The likely ability to sustain a dividend should be analyzed.
   B. Over the life cycle of a company, dividend policy should change.
      1. A token dividend would be expected to be paid early on.
      2. Dividends would increase as relatively fewer productive investment opportunities are found.
      3. A mature company would tend to self liquidate by paying substantial dividends.
   C. A company that is growing and profitable may not be liquid, for its funds may go into fixed assets and permanent current assets, so its ability to pay a dividend may be limited.
   D. The greater the ability of a firm to borrow, the greater its flexibility and ability to pay a cash dividend.
   E. A company whose dividend-payout ratio is out of line with other companies in the industry should be able to justify its position.
   F. A company should analyze what information it is conveying with its present dividend and what it would convey with a possible change in dividend.
   G. If a company pays substantial dividends, it may need to raise capital later through the sale of stock, thereby diluting the controlling interest in the company.
   H. Companies with a low dividend payout which are in danger of being acquired, may establish a high dividend payout to keep existing stockholders from turning control over to "outsiders."
   I. When a firm is closely held, management usually knows the dividend desires of its stockholders and acts accordingly.
   J. The protective covenants in a bond indenture or loan agreement may include a restriction on payment of dividends to preserve the company's ability to service debt.

MULTIPLE CHOICE QUESTIONS

12.1 In order to determine the dividends to be paid under the residual dividend approach, it is necessary to know
   a. net income and the tax rate.
   b. the capital structure, the capital budget, and the tax rate.
   c. the capital structure, the capital budget, and net income.
   d. the capital structure, the capital budget, net income, and the tax rate.

12.2 In a world of perfect capital markets, no flotation costs on securities issued, no taxes, and a given investment policy for the firm, dividends
a. are irrelevant.
b. depend on the capital structure.
c. increase stock price.
d. decrease stock price.

12.3 In the Modigliani-Miller argument, stockholders who don't receive sufficient cash dividends are assumed to
a. borrow.
b. sell some of their stock.
c. diversify.
d. get dividends from other investments.

12.4 By itself, the differential in tax rates on dividends and capital gains should result in dividend paying stocks having _____ expected returns than non-dividend paying stocks.
a. higher before-tax
b. lower before-tax
c. higher after-tax
d. lower after-tax

12.5 Because of different tax situations, non-dividend paying stocks should be preferred by
a. tax exempt financial institutions.
b. corporate investors.
c. low tax rate individual investors.
d. wealthy investors.

12.6 Which of the following is likely to favor dividends rather than earnings retention?
a. flotation costs
b. taxes
c. transaction costs on the sale of securities
d. institutional restrictions

12.7 The financial signaling of dividends is based on
a. investor preference for dividends.
b. investor preference for capital gains.
c. personal taxes.
d. asymmetric information.

12.8 Most ex-dividend day studies have shown that stock prices
a. rise just prior to the ex-dividend date.
b. go down by the amount of the dividend on the ex-dividend date.
c. go down by less than the amount of the dividend on the ex-dividend date.
d. don't change on the ex-dividend date.

12.9 The 1986 Tax Act _____ the "yield tilt."
      a. created
      b. increased
      c. had no effect on
      d. reduced

12.10 Which of the following would tend to decrease a company's
      ability to pay a dividend?
      a. liquidity
      b. protective covenants
      c. corporate maturity
      d. ability to borrow

ANSWERS

12.1	c	p.	327	12.6	d	pp.	334-335
12.2	a	p.	328	12.7	d	pp.	335-336
12.3	b	p.	328	12.8	c	pp.	336-337
12.4	a	pp.	330-331	12.9	d	p.	339
12.5	d	p.	331	12.10	b	pp.	340-341

CHAPTER 13

OTHER ASPECTS OF DIVIDEND POLICY

██

PERSPECTIVE

In addition to the relative amount of dividends paid out, the pattern in which payment is made can be important to investors. It has long been believed that the stability of dividends has a positive effect on the market price of stock.

Other decisions about dividends can also be made. Dividends can be paid in cash or in stock. Both stock dividends and stock splits appear to signal favorable information to the market. Reverse stock splits send a negative signal.

If a firm has more cash than it needs for present and foreseeable future investments, it may distribute these funds either as dividends or by the repurchase of stock. Repurchases can be accomplished either with a tender offer or through purchases in the open market. These also appear to have a positive signaling effect.

There are certain procedures that must be followed when a dividend is declared, and dividend payments are subject to various legal restrictions.

CHAPTER OUTLINE

I. A stock that pays a stable dividend over time may be priced higher than if it pays out a fixed percentage of earnings, even though the long-term total dividends are the same.
   A. Investors may be willing to pay a premium for dividend stability because of the informational content of dividends.
      1. When earnings drop and a company does not cut its dividend, it conveys management's view that the future of the company is better than the drop in earnings suggests.
      2. An increase in a stable dividend indicates that management is reasonably confident that a higher dividend can be maintained.
      3. If there is a downward trend in earnings, a stable dividend will not convey forever the impression of a rosy future.
      4. A stable dividend cannot give the illusion of underlying stability to a company in an unstable business with wide swings in earnings.

B. Investors who desire a specific periodic income will prefer a company with stable dividends. Although they can always sell portions of their stock for income when the dividend is insufficient, they may be averse to dipping into principal and to transaction and inconvenience costs.

C. Companies usually must have an uninterrupted pattern of dividends to be included on various governmental lists of securities in which pension funds, savings banks, trustees, insurance companies, and certain others may invest.

D. Some companies have as policy a long-run target dividend-payout ratio.
   1. When earnings increase to a new level, management does not increase dividends until it feels it can maintain the increase in earnings.
   2. In general, companies are reluctant to cut the absolute amount of their cash dividend.

E. Companies with fluctuating earnings sometimes declare an extra dividend.
   1. This extra dividend enables the company to maintain a stable record of regular dividends but also to distribute to stockholders some of the rewards of prosperity.
   2. If a company pays the same extra dividend annually, it becomes expected and defeats its purpose.

II. Stock dividends and stock splits are only significantly different from an accounting standpoint.

A. A stock dividend is the payment of additional stock to stockholders and does not change their proportional ownership.
   1. It is essentially a recapitalization because the amount of the stock dividend is transferred from retained earnings to the common stock and paid-in capital accounts.
   2. The par value of the stock stays the same.
   3. Earnings per share are diluted but the proportion of total earnings available to each stockholder remains unchanged.
   4. The accounting treatment of large-percentage stock dividends (more than 20 percent of the number of common shares already outstanding) is slightly different: retained earnings are reduced by only the par value of the new shares issued.

B. With a stock split, the number of shares is increased through a proportional reduction in the par value of the stock.
   1. The common stock, paid-in capital, and retained earnings accounts remain unchanged.
   2. The proportional ownership of stockholders does not change.

3. Earnings per share are reduced but the proportion of total earnings available to each stockholder remains unchanged.
4. Stock is split when a company wishes to achieve a substantial reduction in the market price per share.
5. Companies usually increase the total dividends paid to stockholders after a split.
C. Theoretically, a stock dividend or split has no value to investors because their proportional ownership of the company is unchanged.
1. Psychologically, a stock dividend may have a favorable effect on some stockholders because it represent a windfall gain; they can sell it and still retain their original holdings.
2. A stock dividend may be employed to conserve cash as earnings rise, but it involves a lowering of the dividend-payout ratio and sizable administrative costs.
3. Stocks splits and occasionally stock dividends can be used to reduce the price of the stock to a lower, more popular trading range.
   a. The mix of stockholders may change towards increased individual holdings and decreased institutional holdings.
   b. Trading volume tends to increase after a split.
4. A stock dividend or split may be more convincing than a press announcement that management believes the company has favorable future prospects.
   a. Empirical studies have shown that there is a statistically significant and positive stock price reaction around the announcement of a stock dividend or split.
   b. The greater the split, the greater the stock price reaction.
D. A reverse stock split is employed to increase the market price per share when the stock is considered to be selling at too low a price.
1. Many companies have an aversion to seeing their stock fall below $10 per share.
2. Empirical studies have shown that there is a statistically significant and negative stock price reaction around the announcement of a reverse split.

III. If a company has excess cash and insufficient profitable investment opportunities, it may decide to repurchase some of its outstanding common stock instead of paying out a large dividend.
A. There are two common methods of stock repurchase.
1. A tender offer is a formal offer to stockholders to purchase a fixed number of shares at a price above the current market price.
   a. Stockholders can elect either to sell their stock at the specified price or continue to hold it.

81

b. If stockholders tender more shares than the company seeks, it may elect to purchase all, part, or none of the excess.
c. It is used when the company seeks a large amount of stock.

2. The company may purchase its own stock in the open market.
a. It usually negotiates the brokerage fee.
b. If the repurchase program is gradual, it drives up the price of the stock.
c. The company's intentions must be announced.

B. With repurchase, fewer shares remain outstanding, so earnings, dividends, and market price per share should rise.

1. The investor's capital gain from repurchase should equal the dividend that otherwise would have been paid.

2. The repurchase price per share should be such that shareholders who do not tender will be no better or worse off than shareholders who tender, and vice versa.

3. The price the company should offer is
$P* = (S)(P_c)/(S - n)$, where
$P*$ = equilibrium share repurchase price,
S = number of shares outstanding prior to the distribution,
P_c = current market price per share prior to the distribution,
n = number of shares to be repurchased.

4. The repurchase of stock offers a tax advantage over payment of dividends to the taxpaying investor.

5. Share repurchase offers the investor a timing option which is not available when a cash dividend is paid.

6. If a company undertakes a steady program of repurchase instead of paying dividends, the Internal Revenue Service will consider the program as providing dividend income and will disallow a claim of capital gains.

C. The repurchase of shares has been regarded as an investment decision, a financing decision, and a dividend decision.

1. It is not an investment decision because no company can exist by investing only in its own stock.

2. It may be a financing decision if its purpose is to alter the capital structure of the firm by issuing debt and using the money to repurchase stock.

3. It may be a dividend decision if its purpose is to distribute excess cash to the shareholders in place of a large dividend payment.

D. If management believes the stock is undervalued and refrains from tendering its own individually-owned shares, empirical studies show that repurchase announcement sends a positive signal to the market.

IV. The declaration of dividends involves certain procedures, and their payment is subject to various legal restrictions.

A. When the board of directors declares a cash dividend, it specifies a date of record.
   1. Stockholders who are on the stock transfer books of the company at the close of business that day are entitled to the dividend.
   2. Those who come on the books afterwards are not.
   3. The brokerage community has a rule whereby new stockholders are entitled to dividends only if they buy the stock more than 4 business days before the date of record.
   4. The date that is 4 business days before the date of record is known as the ex-dividend date.
   5. Once a dividend is declared, it must be paid; the declared but unpaid dividend is a current liability.
B. Some legal restrictions influence dividend policy.
   1. To protect creditors, most states prohibit the payment of dividends if these dividends impair capital (the par value of the common stock in some states, the par value plus paid-in capital in others).
   2. Some states prohibit the payment of cash dividends if the company is insolvent.
      a. Legal insolvency means that liabilities exceed assets.
      b. Technical insolvency means that the firm is unable to pay its creditors as obligations come due.
   3. The Internal Revenue Code prohibits the undue retention of earnings, which usually means the building up of a substantial liquid position significantly in excess of the present and future investment needs of the company.

MULTIPLE CHOICE QUESTIONS

13.1 A company with a stable dividend policy should
   a. be higher-priced than a company with a constant dividend payout ratio.
   b. have a higher dividend yield than a company with a constant dividend payout ratio.
   c. have stable earnings per share.
   d. attract few institutional investors.

13.2 A stock dividend
   a. is equal to a cash dividend.
   b. increases retained earnings.
   c. decreases retained earnings.
   d. reduces the par value of the common stock.

13.3 A stock dividend is more likely to result in a stock price increase when
   a. the dividend percentage is large.
   b. the cash dividend is decreased.
   c. the cash dividend is increased.
   d. the overall stock market is falling.

13.4   A stock split
        a. increases retained earnings.
        b. increases the market price of the common stock.
        c. decreases retained earnings.
        d. decreases the par value of the common stock.

13.5   A reverse stock split
        a. increases retained earnings.
        b. increases the market price of the common stock.
        c. decreases retained earnings.
        d. decreases the par value of the common stock.

The following information applies to questions 13.6 and 13.7.
The ABC company has 100,000 shares of $10 par common stock
outstanding.   The stock has a market price of $50 per share.   The
earnings per share are $5.04.

13.6   After a 5 percent stock dividend, the earnings per share will
        be approximately
        a. $5.29.
        b. $5.00.
        c. $4.80.
        d. $4.60.

13.7   After a 5 percent stock dividend, the market price of the
        stock should be approximately
        a. $40.00.
        b. $47.62.
        c. $50.00.
        d. $52.50.

13.8   The benefit arising from a stock repurchase rather than a
        cash dividend payment is
        a. a timing option is given to the investor.
        b. earnings per share decrease.
        c. the price earnings ratio decreases.
        d. total company earnings increase.

13.9   Repurchase by a firm of its own stock
        a. is illegal.
        b. is risky.
        c. can only be done by a tender offer.
        d. can be used to quickly increase its debt-equity ratio.

13.10 The ex-dividend date is
        a. the date of record.
        b. 4 business days before the date of record.
        c. 4 business days after the date of record.
        d. 4 business days before the date of payment.

ANSWERS

13.1	a	pp.	351-352
13.2	c	pp.	354-355
13.3	c	p.	355
13.4	d	pp.	355-356
13.5	b	pp.	358-359
13.6	c	pp.	354-355

$5.04/1.05 = $4.80

13.7	b	pp.	354-355
13.8	a	pp.	360-361
13.9	d	p.	359
13.10	b	p.	363

$50/1.05 = $47.62

CHAPTER 14

WORKING CAPITAL MANAGEMENT
AND EFFICIENT MARKET CONSIDERATIONS

PERSPECTIVE

In theory, it does not make sense to separate decisions involving specific current assets and liabilities from the overall investment and financing decisions of the firm. In practice, certain characteristics associated with current assets differentiate them somewhat from fixed assets.

The theoretical justification for maintaining liquidity (holding cash and marketable securities) rests primarily on the presence of bankruptcy costs. Receivables and inventory can be evaluated in much the same manner as fixed assets by using a single-factor or multi-factor valuation model. The amount of current liabilities the firm maintains is a by-product of fundamental decisions involving capital structure and the maturity and other conditions of the debt.

The chapter concludes that the "working capital" of the firm is not managed. Specific decisions are made affecting specific types of current assets and current liabilities.

CHAPTER OUTLINE

I. Working capital management usually involves the administration of current assets and current liabilities.
   A. In practice, working capital management consists of optimizing the levels of cash, marketable securities, receivables and inventories without reference to the overall valuation of the firm.
   B. Recently developed models for cash, receivables, and inventory management balance the benefits of a particular level of current assets against the risk-adjusted cost of maintaining it.

II. Current asset decisions must be made with respect to the overall valuation of the firm.
   A. Liquid assets is a term used to describe money and assets that are readily convertible into money.
      1. Liquidity has two dimensions:
         a. the time necessary to convert the asset into money,
         b. the degree of certainty associated with the price realized for the asset.

2. The most liquid assets of the firm are cash and marketable securities.
3. Under the assumptions of perfect capital markets, excess cash cannot be justified.
    a. If the company cannot employ its funds in projects providing expected returns no less than those required by the financial markets, such excess liquidity should be distributed.
    b. If the firm becomes technically insolvent, creditors will be able to step in instantaneously and liquidate assets, run the company themselves, or effect a costless reorganization.
4. In imperfect markets, liquidity may become a desirable characteristic affecting value.
    a. A company can reduce the probability of bankruptcy and lower the expected value of bankruptcy costs by maintaining liquidity.
    b. The cost of liquidity is the differential in interest earned on the investment of funds in liquid assets and the cost of financing these assets.
    c. If a company had immediate access to external financing which involved no flotation costs, it could avoid or at least reduce the possibility of bankruptcy, thereby eliminating the need for liquid assets.
B. Receivables and inventories should be evaluated from the same perspective as fixed assets, although they are analyzed in terms of overall levels instead of specific assets.
1. Projects that are composed entirely of receivables or inventories can be analyzed using a market valuation approach.
    a. The appropriate discount rate is the risk-free rate plus a risk premium to capture the unavoidable (systematic) risk of the project.
    b. Risk may be due to one factor as in the CAPM or to multiple factors, as in the APT model.
    c. The required return on investment increases with the amount of systematic risk in the project.
2. Market imperfections may require that a total-firm risk approach be used as well.
    a. Because receivables are a financial asset rather than a real asset, there should be fewer imperfections involved with receivable investment than with inventory investment.
    b. There may be somewhat fewer imperfections in the product market for inventories than in that for fixed assets.

III. The active component of current liabilities should be determined by decisions involving the composition and terms of the company's debt, given the level of debt established by the capital structure decision.

A. Current liabilities **have** two components.
  1. The passive component consists of payables and accruals which change relative to changes in the level of production or services offered.
  2. The active component consists of debt whose terms and conditions result from specific financing decisions.

B. In perfect and complete financial markets, decisions about the maturity, collateral, coupon rate, specific features, protective covenants, domestic/foreign lenders, and other features of debt would be irrelevant.
  1. A perfect market is characterized by the absence of:
    a. taxes,
    b. bankruptcy costs,
    c. transaction costs,
    d. information costs and delays,
    e. restrictions on market participants.
  2. A complete market contains a distinct marketable security corresponding to every contingency in the world.
  3. In a perfect and complete financial market, all of a company's financial liabilities would have the same cost on a certainty-equivalent basis; there would be no reward for variety of debt instrument.

C. Since financial markets are both imperfect and incomplete, a company may be able to lower its interest cost by packaging debt instruments to appeal to certain clientele and by taking advantage of imperfections.
  1. A reasonable amount of research has been done on the call feature, the maturity structure of debt, and on the coupon-rate effect.
  2. Little research has been done on the effect of different types of secured positions and various protective covenants on the value of debt.

MULTIPLE CHOICE QUESTIONS

14.1 Sophisticated models balancing the benefits of a current asset level against the risk-adjusted cost of maintaining it have been developed for all of the following except
  a. cash.
  b. receivables.
  c. payables.
  d. inventories.

14.2 The major market imperfection which might cause liquidity management to be of value is
  a. taxes.
  b. transactions costs.
  c. flotation costs.
  d. bankruptcy costs.

14.3 The cost of additional liquidity is determined by
   a. the cost of borrowing.
   b. the cost of lending.
   c. the cost of borrowing less the cost of lending.
   d. the reduction in the probability of bankruptcy.

14.4 The optimal level of liquidity should be determined by
   a. a cost-benefit analysis.
   b. minimizing bankruptcy costs.
   c. minimizing the probability of bankruptcy.
   d. minimizing borrowing costs.

14.5 According to the assumptions of the CAPM, an investment in receivables should have
   a. a return greater than the investment in inventory.
   b. the same required return, regardless of the firm undertaking it.
   c. a return based on its residual risk.
   d. a return based on its total risk.

14.6 In general, there are probably fewest market imperfections involved with an investment in which of the following?
   a. receivables
   b. inventories
   c. machinery
   d. buildings

14.7 A complete financial market is one in which
   a. both debt and equity are issued.
   b. the desires of investors with respect to kinds of securities offered are satisfied.
   c. firms have the incentive to tailor the debt they issue in order to lower their cost.
   d. risk-adjusted rates of return on securities would lie below the SML.

14.8 Under the assumptions of perfect and complete capital markets
   a. liquidity management is an important managerial tool.
   b. if a firm becomes technically insolvent, creditors can adjust instantaneously.
   c. firms will tailor debt to take advantage of unfulfilled investor desires.
   d. long-term debt will be more advantageous to the firm than short-term debt.

14.9 At times, the existence of a market imperfection relative to _____ can justify the existence of the _____ condition of debt.
   a. flotation costs, sinking fund
   b. bankruptcy costs, call feature
   c. clientele effect, zero-coupon
   d. information costs, secured

14.10 Working capital
  a. management is important in a world of perfect capital markets.
  b. is the result of an important active decision made by management in which the amount of working capital is specifically determined.
  c. is independent of the decisions concerning the maturity composition and other characteristics of the firm's debt.
  d. management is a misnomer because working capital is not really managed.

ANSWERS

14.1	c	p.	374		14.6	a	p.	379
14.2	d	p.	376		14.7	b	p.	378
14.3	c	p.	378		14.8	b	pp.	380-381
14.4	a	p.	378		14.9	c	p.	381
14.5	b	p.	379		14.10	d	pp.	382-383

CHAPTER 15

MANAGEMENT OF CASH AND MARKETABLE SECURITIES

PERSPECTIVE

In managing liquid assets, corporations must consider their transactions and precautionary motives. When managing cash, they attempt to accelerate collections and slow down disbursements. There are various methods available for accomplishing these ends.

When dividing its total liquid assets between cash and marketable securities, the firm must determine the optimal level of cash. The residual is invested in marketable securities. The optimal level of cash is the greater of compensating balances required by banks or a self-imposed minimum balance. The size of this balance can be determined by use of EOQ, stochastic, or probabilistic models, or by simpler decision rules.

When investing in marketable securities, the company must make decisions about the default risk, marketability, maturity, coupon rate, taxability, and option-type features that it is willing to incorporate into its portfolio. It then selects from a substantial list of available money market instruments. These securities do not offer the diversification advantages that are available from investment in common stocks, so managing the marketable securities portfolio is significantly different from managing a stock portfolio.

CHAPTER OUTLINE

I. If efficiently managed, investment in specific current assets can contribute to shareholder wealth.
   A. There are three motives for holding cash and marketable securities.
      1. The transactions motive is the need for cash to meet payments arising in the ordinary course of business.
      2. The precautionary motive has to do with maintaining a cushion or buffer to meet unexpected contingencies.
         a. The more predictable the cash flows of the business, the smaller the precautionary balance needed.
         b. The greater the ready borrowing power of the company to meet emergency cash drains, the smaller the precautionary balance needed.
      3. The speculative motive is the holding of cash to take advantage of expected changes in security prices.

91

a. When interest rates are expected to rise and security prices to fall, the firm should hold cash until the rise in interest rates ceases.

b. When interest rates are expected to fall, cash may be invested in securities.

B. Cash management involves managing the monies of the firm in order to maximize cash availability and interest income on any idle funds.

1. The treasurer's office usually manages cash.

2. The cash budget is the basic tool for calculating the likely availability of cash, as well as the timing and magnitude of future cash balances.

3. Preparing multiple cash budgets under alternative assumptions is the best way to take uncertainty into account.

4. Daily or even more frequent bank reports are needed on:

a. cash balances in each bank account,

b. the cash disbursed,

c. the average daily collected balances,

d. the marketable security position of the firm,

e. detailed changes in this position.

II. The overall efficiency of cash management depends on the various collection and disbursement methods of the firm.

A. Acceleration of collections means reducing the time between when customers pay their bills and when the checks become usable funds for the firm. This time has three components:

1. the mailing time of payments from customers to the company;

2. the time during which payments received by the firm remain uncollected funds. This float consists of:

a. the time it takes a company to process checks internally,

b. the time consumed in clearing the check through the banking system;

3. the time it takes to move funds to disbursement banks.

B. There are various methods to reduce some or all of these components of collection time.

1. There are three ways of moving funds among banks.

a. Wire transfer, which costs about $10, immediately transfers funds from one bank to another through Fedwire, Western Union Bank Wire, or CHIPS.

b. Depository transfer checks cost about fifty cents, are drawn on the local bank, payable to a concentration bank, and are collected through the usual channels involving delays of 2 or more days.

c. Electronic transfer checks through automatic clearinghouses make funds available one business day later.

2. Concentration banking is the establishment of multiple collection centers to serve customers in particular geographic areas.

a. Each center bills customers in its area, makes daily deposits of payments received in its local bank, and transfers surplus funds to a concentration bank with which the company has a disbursement account.

b. The alternative, one collection center at company headquarters, can add days to the collection time.

c. The funds made available for investment elsewhere equal the average daily customer remittances times the number of days saved.

d. Profits from the investment of the released funds must be compared with the additional costs of a decentralized system.

3. A lock-box arrangement eliminates the time between the receipt of remittances by the company and their deposit in the bank.

a. The company rents a local post office box and has customers mail remittances to it.

b. The local bank picks up the mail several times a day, records the checks and deposits them in the company's account.

c. The company receives a deposit slip, a list of payments, and any material from the customers included in the mailing envelope.

d. Because the cost is almost directly proportional to the number of checks deposited, lock-boxes are usually not profitable if the average remittance is small.

4. When a small number of remittances account for a large proportion of total deposits, these checks may be profitably subjected to special handling.

5. A company that has a bank account in every city where it has either a sales office or a production facility might be able to reduce cash balances considerably if it were to eliminate some of these accounts.

6. Using the date of receipt of a remittance instead of the postmark date to determine whether a payment qualifies for a discount usually accelerates collections.

C. The objective in managing disbursements is to slow them down as much as possible.

1. A company with multiple banks should be able to shift funds quickly to banks from which disbursements are made, to prevent excessive balances from building up temporarily in collections banks.

2. Funds transferred to disbursement banks should be used either to pay bills or to invest in marketable securities.

3. If cash discounts are taken on accounts payable, the loss of discounts due to clerical inefficiencies should be eliminated or at least minimized.

4. Payments should be made on the due dates, not before.

5. Paying with drafts instead of ordinary checks slows down the disbursements but usually involves a higher service charge from the banks.
6. A company can "play the float" by locating disbursement banks in a way that maximizes the time a check will remain outstanding.
7. Many companies maintain a separate account for payroll disbursements.
   a. Since not all paychecks are cashed on payday, the company need not have funds on deposit to cover its entire payroll on that day.
   b. Based on experience, the company can construct a distribution of when checks will be presented for collection.
8. A similar process can be used with a separate account for dividends.
9. If a company has multiple disbursement accounts, they may be set up as zero balance accounts (ZBAs).
   a. One master disbursing account contains the balance specified by the bank; it will probably be less than the sum of the balances that would have been required for the multiple disbursement accounts if they were not ZBAs.
   b. At the end of each day, the bank automatically transfers just enough funds from the master account to each of the ZBAs to cover the checks presented to them for collection.

III. The above procedures are gradually being replaced with an electronic funds transfer system (EFT).
   A. At the retail level, individuals can use plastic cards with magnetic coding.
      1. In dealing with banks, these cards can be used to obtain cash, to transfer funds from one account to another, to pay bills, to borrow, and so forth.
      2. Such a card can be used to pay for purchases at stores.
   B. Retailers can also use "smart cards" to guarantee a customer's check.
   C. In intercompany transactions, EFTs can be used to pay suppliers, deposit payrolls automatically in employee accounts, pay taxes, and make dividend and other payments.
   D. The use of EFTs allows tighter control over disbursements and usually improves supplier relations, but it eliminates float.
   E. Several factors affect the cost of EFTs.
      1. The cost per transaction is reduced as volume increases.
      2. The service charge over time has been reduced by the intense competition among financial institutions and large retailers who provide financial services.
      3. The higher the interest rate, the greater the opportunity cost of holding cash and the more attractive EFT techniques become.

IV. Given the overall level of transactions and precautionary balances, management must decide on the appropriate split between cash and marketable securities.
   A. The level of cash, which determines the level of marketable securities, should be set by the greater of the following two constraints:
      1. the compensating balance requirements of the company's banks.
         a. Banks set their minimum average level of cash balances required at the point at which the bank's income from the account just equals the costs of the account.
         b. Some banks will require the payment of cash fees for services rendered instead of the maintenance of compensating balances.
      2. a self-imposed constraint determined by the need for cash, the predictability of this need, the interest rate on marketable securities, and the fixed cost of effecting a transfer between marketable securities and cash.
   B. If transactions and inconvenience costs were zero and conversion between cash and marketable securities were instantaneous, the firm would hold no cash.
   C. If the future were known with certainty, projected cash would be invested as long as the interest earnings exceeded transactions and inconvenience costs, and as long as the delays in conversion between cash and marketable securities did not hinder the firm in paying its bills.
   D. If the cash flows of the firm are known with certainty, the economic order quantity formula (EOQ) used in inventory management could be used for determining the optimal average amount of transaction cash.
      1. The model balances the carrying cost of holding cash (the interest forgone on marketable securities) against the fixed cost of transferring marketable securities to cash or vice versa.
      2. The total cost of a cash balance can be defined as
      Total Cost = $b(T/C) + i(C/2)$, where
         b   = fixed cost of a transaction, independent of the amount transferred,
         T   = total demand for cash for the period,
         C   = cash balance,
         i   = interest rate on marketable securities, assumed to be constant,
         C/2 = average cash balance.
      3. If the derivative of total cost with respect to C is set equal to zero, the optimal level of cash is
      $C* = (2bT/i)^{1/2}$.
      4. The EOQ model assumes that cash payments are steady over the time period involved, but it can also be applied when receipts are continuous and there are discrete large payments.

5. If cash payments are not completely predictable but the degree of uncertainty is modest, the financial manager need only add a cushion so that a transfer from marketable securities to cash is triggered at some level of cash above zero.

E. If the uncertainty of cash payments is large but cash balances fluctuate randomly, the financial manager can apply control theory to the problem and use a stochastic model.

1. Control limits can be set so that when cash reaches an upper limit, a transfer of cash to marketable securities is made, and when it hits a lower limit, a transfer from marketable securities to cash is triggered.

2. As long as the cash balance stays between the upper and lower limits, no transactions take place.

3. The Miller-Orr model is a relatively simple application of control theory. It sets h as the upper bound, zero as the lower bound, and z as the return point.

4. The optimal value of z is
   $z = (3b\sigma^2/4i)^{1/3}$, where,
      b = fixed cost associated with a security transaction,
      σ = standard deviation of daily net cash flows,
      i = interest rate per day on marketable securities.

5. The optimal value of h is 3z. When the cash balance reaches h, (h - z) dollars of marketable securities are bought, and the new balance becomes z dollars.

6. When the cash balance reaches zero, z dollars of marketable securities are sold, and the new balance becomes z dollars.

7. The average cash balance cannot be determined exactly in advance, but it is approximately (z + h)/3.

8. The higher the fixed cost of a security transaction, and/or the lower the interest rate, the further apart the control limits will be.

F. When cash flows are neither reasonably predictable nor reasonably unpredictable, a probabilistic approach may be employed.

1. For various possible cash flow outcomes, the expected net earnings associated with different initial levels of marketable securities can be determined.

2. The expected net earnings is the gross interest earned on the marketable security position less the expected fixed cost of selling securities to meet a cash shortfall and less the expected loss of interest income associated with the sale of those securities.

3. The optimal level of marketable securities is the level at which expected net earnings are maximized.

G. If none of the three optimization models (EOQ, stochastic, or probability) offers improvement over simpler decision rules, the simpler rules should be used.

V. Once the firm has determined an optimal cash balance, the residual of its liquid assets is invested in marketable securities.
   A. The accounting practice is to list marketable securities and time deposits as "cash equivalents" on the balance sheet if their original maturity is 3 months or less, and as "short-term investments" if their maturity is more than 3 months but less than one year.
   B. Yields on marketable securities vary, depending on their:
      1. default risk, which is the probability that the borrower will not make principal and/or interest payments when due.
         a. The greater the default risk of the borrower, the higher the yield.
         b. For all practical purposes, Treasury securities and U.S. government agency issues are default free.
         c. Most other securities are rated by Moody's Investors Service and Standard & Poor's.
      2. marketability, which is the ability to sell a significant volume of securities in a short period of time without significant price concession.
         a. The more marketable the security, the greater the ability to execute a large transaction near the quoted price.
         b. The less marketable the security, the higher the yield.
      3. length of time to maturity.
         a. For any specific type of security, a yield curve can be obtained by plotting time to maturity on the X-axis and yield on the Y-axis.
         b. The yield curve is usually upward-sloping.
         c. In general, the longer the maturity, the greater the risk of fluctuation in the market price of the security, and the higher the yield.
         d. When interest rates are expected to fall significantly, the yield curve tends to be downward-sloping.
      4. coupon rate.
         a. The lower the coupon rate, the greater the price change for a given shift in interest rates.
         b. With lower coupons, more of the total return to the investor is reflected in the principal payment at maturity as opposed to the interim interest payments.
         c. "Riding the yield curve" refers to a policy of taking advantage of an upward-sloping yield curve by selling securities before they mature.
            1. If interest rates are expected to fall, a company invests in long-term securities with low coupon rates, because these securities will enjoy the greatest increase in market price.

97

2. If interest rates are expected to rise, a company invests in short-term securities with high coupon rates, because these securities will incur the smallest decline in market price.
5. taxability at both federal and state levels.
    a. Interest income from state and local government securities is tax exempt, lowering their yield.
    b. For corporations located in states with income taxes, interest income on Treasury securities is exempt from state income taxes.
6. option-type features.
    a. An option which links the debt security to equity, such as a conversion privilege or a warrant, lowers the yield.
    b. An option which allows or requires the company to prepay some or all of the debt, such as a call feature or a sinking fund, raises the yield.
C. The vast majority of corporations invest in money market instruments which are highly marketable, subject to little default risk, and mature in less than a year.
    1. U.S. Treasury bills (maturity of 1 year or less), notes (maturity of 1 to 10 years) and bonds (maturity greater than 10 years) are the safest and most marketable investments, but provide the lowest yield.
    2. A repurchase agreement, or "repo," is the sale of short-term Treasury securities by a government securities dealer to a corporation, with an agreement to buy the security back in the near future (in one or more days, as desired by the investor).
    3. Agency securities are both short- and long-term obligations issued by various agencies of the federal government, and are not guaranteed by the Treasury, but cannot fail for political reasons.
    4. Bankers' acceptances are drafts that are accepted by banks and are used in financing foreign and domestic trade. They are discount securities and generally have maturities of less than 6 months.
    5. Commercial paper consists of short-term unsecured promissory notes issued by finance companies and certain industrial corporations.
        a. It can be sold directly to the public by the issuer or through dealers.
        b. It is sold on a discount basis, and maturities generally range from 30 to 270 days.
        c. There is essentially no secondary market, although issuers and dealers may repurchase the paper on request.
    6. Negotiable certificates of deposit (CDs) result from the deposit of at least $100,000 at a commercial bank for a specified period of time (generally 30 to 360 days) and at a specified rate of interest. A good secondary

market has developed for the CDs of the large money market banks.

7. Eurodollars are deposits of at least $100,000 in foreign banks or in foreign branches of U.S. banks.
   a. The market is international and therefore free of government regulation.
   b. The rates quoted on deposits vary according to the maturity of the deposit, but the rates on loans depend on maturity and default risk.
   c. For a given maturity, the lending rate always exceeds the deposit rate.
   d. The benchmark rate is the 6-month London interbank offered rate (LIBOR), the rate at which banks make loans to each other.
   e. Call money deposits are available, allowing investors to get their money back on demand.

8. Short-term municipals are a commercial paper type of instrument whose interest rate is reset every week so that the variation in market price is minimized. They are much more marketable than municipal notes and bonds.

9. Money market preferred stock is a special type of preferred stock for which an auction is held every 49 days.
   a. The auction provides the investor with liquidity and relative price stability but does not protect from default risk.
   b. The auction rate is usually a fraction of the commercial paper rate.
   c. In a failed auction where there are insufficient bidders, there is a default dividend rate for one period that is frequently 110 percent of the commercial paper rate, and the holder has the option to redeem the instrument at its face value.

10. The hedged dividend capture usually involves buying preferred stock right before a dividend is to be paid and simultaneously writing a call option on the stock.

D. Based on an evaluation of expected net cash flows and the uncertainty associated with these cash flows, the decision to invest excess cash in marketable securities involves not only the amount to invest but also the type of security in which to invest.

1. If future cash-flow patterns are known with reasonable certainty and the yield curve is upward-sloping, a company should choose securities that will mature approximately when the funds will be needed, allowing the firm to pursue securities that will maximize the yield on the portfolio.

2. If the yield curve is downward-sloping, a company should invest in securities having maturities shorter than the intended holding period, then reinvest at maturity.

3. If future cash flows are fairly uncertain, the company must attempt to balance marketability, risk with respect

to fluctuations in market value, and transaction costs.
4. The larger the security portfolio, the more diverse the portfolio can be, and the greater the number of people responsible for managing it.
5. For multinational companies, cash and marketable securities may be kept in multiple currencies.
6. Since there is a high degree of correlation in the price movements of money market instruments over time, diversification to reduce the dispersion of possible returns from a portfolio is difficult to achieve.

MULTIPLE CHOICE QUESTIONS

15.1 The primary motives for a corporation to hold cash are
a. transactions and speculative.
b. transactions and precautionary.
c. precautionary and speculative.
d. transactions, precautionary, and speculative.

15.2 The quickest means of transferring funds from one bank to another is
a. wire transfer.
b. depository transfer checks.
c. electronic transfer checks through automatic clearing-houses.
d. paper checks cleared through the Federal Reserve System.

15.3 The processing cost is greatest for
a. wire transfers.
b. depository transfer checks.
c. electronic transfer checks through automatic clearing-houses.
d. paper checks cleared through the Federal Reserve System.

15.4 BBB Company is considering establishing a lock-box system. It is anticipated that its use will accelerate the availability of the average daily collections of $40,000 by 3 days. The opportunity rate on funds invested in marketable securities is 9 percent. The annual cost of using the system is $8,000. The net benefit (cost) of the lock-box plan is
a. ($5,400).
b. $2,800.
c. $5,400.
d. $10,800.

15.5 The use of electronic funds transfers
a. eliminates float.
b. permits tighter control over disbursements.
c. may reduce servicing costs.
d. all of the above.

15.6 In the EOQ model approach to determining optimal cash, the amount of cash a firm will hold is positively related to _____ and inversely related to _____.
a. interest rate on marketable securities, total cash needed during the period
b. total cash needed during the period, fixed cost per transfer
c. fixed cost per transfer, interest rate on marketable securities
d. interest rate on marketable securities, fixed cost per transfer

15.7 Which of the following is least likely to be in a corporation's portfolio of marketable securities?
a. newly issued U.S. Treasury bills
b. newly issued corporate bonds
c. certificates of deposit
d. short-term agency securities

15.8 When an investor is "riding the yield curve," he
a. plans to hold all securities to maturity.
b. buys securities with high coupon rates if interest rates are expected to fall.
c. buys long-term securities when the interest rate cycle has bottomed out.
d. buys very short-term securities when interest rates are expected to rise.

15.9 The type of money market security with the greatest marketability is
a. the negotiable certificate of deposit.
b. a U.S. Treasury bill.
c. the bankers' acceptance.
d. commercial paper.

15.10 The primary reason money market preferred stock is considered in a portfolio of marketable securities for a corporation is related to
a. default risk.
b. marketability.
c. maturity.
d. taxability.

ANSWERS

15.1	b	p.	388		15.6	c	pp.	399-400
15.2	a	p.	390		15.7	b	p.	405
15.3	a	p.	390		15.8	d	p.	405
15.4	b	p.	391		15.9	b	pp.	407-409

($40,000)(3)(0.09) - $8,000 = $2,800

15.5 d p. 396   15.10 d p. 410

CHAPTER 16

MANAGEMENT OF ACCOUNTS RECEIVABLE
AND INVENTORIES

PERSPECTIVE

Accounts receivable management requires that decisions be made with respect to the quality of credit accounts accepted, the credit period extended, the cash discount given, the inclusion of special terms, and the level of collection expenditures. Each decision involves a trade-off between profitability and cost. In evaluating a credit applicant, the credit analyst obtains financial and other information about the applicant, analyzes it, and decides if credit should be extended. If repeat orders are expected, a decision must be made about the size of the credit line to be offered.

Inventory management balances the benefits of economies of purchasing, efficiencies in production scheduling, and satisfaction of product demand against the cost of carrying inventory. Of particular concern is the cost of funds invested in inventory. Inventory control is usually accomplished by using mathematical models, one of which is the economic order quantity. This model determines the optimal order size by balancing the ordering costs and carrying costs of the inventory. Its assumption of certainty can be eased by carrying a safety stock.

CHAPTER OUTLINE

I. Economic conditions and the credit policies of the company and its competitors are the chief influences on the level of a company's accounts receivables.
   A. Theoretically, the firm should lower its quality standard for trade accounts accepted as long as the profitability of the sales generated exceeds the added costs of the receivables.
      1. These added costs include:
         a. additional personnel,
         b. the clerical work of checking new accounts and servicing the added volume of receivables,
         c. the increased probability of bad-debt losses,
         d. the opportunity cost of the additional receivables.
      2. The profitability of the sales generated is calculated as the contribution margin (selling price per unit less variable cost per unit) times the number of additional units sold.

102

3. The added costs of the receivables is calculated as the investment in increased accounts receivable (the increase in receivables times the ratio of variable cost to selling price) times the required rate of return on the investment.
4. There are many practical problems in making these estimates, for instance:
    a. the profitability of additional sales, the additional demand for products caused by the relaxed credit standards, and the change in the speed of collections are guesstimates.
    b. changes in capacity utilization may change variable cost per unit.
    c. increased demand may require increased investment in inventories, plant, and/or equipment.
    d. the increase in demand may not be permanent if it induces reaction by competitors.
B. Credit terms involve both the length of the credit period and the cash discount given.
  1. The term "2/10, net 30" means that a 2 percent discount is given if the bill is paid before the tenth day after the date of invoice; payment is due by the thirtieth day.
  2. A change in the terms to 2/10, net 60 will both
     a. increase sales and therefore increase receivables,
     b. slow down collections on the sales that would have occurred anyway and therefore increase receivables.
  3. A change in the terms to 3/10, net 30 may have several consequences.
     a. It will speed up the payment of receivables.
     b. It may increase demand if it is perceived as a price cut to customers who take discounts.
     c. It may reduce bad-debt losses slightly.
C. Seasonal datings can be used to increase demand
  1. by postponing payment until the customer's seasonal cash inflow makes payment convenient for him,
  2. in slack sales seasons and therefore minimize inventory carrying costs.
D. The collection program of the firm usually consists of attempts to collect from overdue accounts by means of letters, phone calls, and/or personal visits, followed by legal action and/or use of a collection agency.
  1. The greater the relative amount spent on collection procedures, the lower the proportion of bad-debt losses and the shorter the average collection period.
  2. The level of sales may be adversely affected by the collection effort expended.
E. For most policy variables, profits increase at a decreasing rate up to a point, and then decrease as the change in policy becomes extreme.

F. Because most of the policy variables are interdependent, sensitivity analysis should be used to determine the optimal set of variable levels.

II. The credit evaluation procedure for individual potential customers involves three related steps.
   A. Information must be obtained about the credit applicant.
      1. There is a tradeoff between the time and cost of obtaining information and the expected profitability of the credit account.
      2. At the very least, the seller may request a financial statement from the applicant.
         a. Refusal to provide a statement probably indicates a weak financial position.
         b. Audited statements are preferable.
         c. Interim as well as year-end figures are desirable for applicants having seasonal sales patterns.
      3. Credit ratings are available, for a price, from various services such as Dun & Bradstreet, Inc., and TRW, Inc.
      4. The seller's bank may obtain a credit check from the bank in which the credit applicant has an account.
      5. Useful information about the character, collateral, capital, and capacity of the management of a potential customer may be available from other suppliers, trade organizations, or credit manager networks.
      6. In general, the riskier the applicant, the greater the desire for more information; but the amount of information collected should be related to the expected profit from an order and the cost of investigation.
   B. The information obtained must be analyzed relative to a minimum quality standard.
      1. Ratio analysis of the applicant's financial statements is of great interest.
      2. The character and strength of the applicant and its management must be considered, as well as the business risk of the company.
      3. Discriminant analysis, numerical rating systems, and expert systems software may be used to filter out obviously good and obviously bad credit applicants, freeing credit analysts to concentrate on marginal applicants.
   C. A credit decision must consider whether repeat sales are likely.
      1. For an initial sale, the decision must be made whether or not to ship the goods and extend credit.
      2. If repeat sales are likely, a line of credit may be established for an account.
         a. A line of credit is a maximum limit on the amount the seller will permit to be owed at any one time.
         b. Likely profits from present and future sales must be balanced against the likely collection period,

collection costs, and probability of bad-debt losses over time.

    c. The line must be reevaluated periodically in order to keep abreast of developments in the account.

  3. Computer-based credit management keeps essential information up to date.

    a. It can provide status reports that summarize all billings, payments, discounts taken, and amounts still owed, per customer.

    b. It can produce an aging of accounts receivable, calculate the average collection period, and display a collection matrix.

    c. It can highlight changes in customer payment behavior before developing problems become serious.

    d. It can prepare special reports for categorization or comparisons of customer accounts by size, industry group, seasonal patterns, or payment experience with the seller.

III. Inventories may be categorized as raw materials, work in process, goods in transit, and finished goods, and are essential in providing flexibility and efficiency.

  A. The benefits of increased inventories are:

    1. efficient production scheduling and utilization of resources,

    2. possible quantity discounts on large purchases of raw materials,

    3. production schedules freed from the vagaries of sales,

    4. the ability to fill orders quickly and retain customers for future sales.

  B. The costs of increased inventories are:

    1. the storage and handling costs associated with holding inventory,

    2. the required return on capital tied up in inventory,

    3. the danger of obsolescence.

  C. Inventories can be controlled by use of mathematical models such as the EOQ.

    1. The economic order quantity (EOQ) determines the optimal order (purchase or production) quantity for a particular item of inventory, given its forecasted usage, ordering cost, and carrying cost.

    2. Use of the EOQ assumes that:

      a. demand for the item is known with certainty,

      b. the item's usage is constant or steady throughout the time period being analyzed,

      c. ordering costs are constant, regardless of the size of the order,

      d. carrying costs, which include the cost of inventory storage, handling, and insurance, as well as the required rate of return on investment, are constant per unit of inventory during the time period,

      e. inventory orders are filled without delay.

3. Total inventory costs are calculated as
   $T = (CQ/2) + (SO/Q)$, where,
      C = carrying costs per period, per unit of
          inventory,
      Q = quantity in units ordered,
      S = total usage of the item per period, in units,
      O = number of orders per period.
4. The greater the quantity ordered, the higher the carrying cost $(CQ/2)$ and the lower the ordering cost (SO/Q). These costs must be balanced.
5. Taking the derivative of T with respect to Q, setting the derivative equal to zero, and solving for Q*, produces the optimal ordering quantity which will minimize total inventory costs:
   $Q* = (2SO/C)^{1/2}$.
6. If there is a delay between when inventory is ordered and when it can be received, but this delay (D = number of days of "lead time") is constant and known with certainty, then the firm need only calculate the number of days between orders (N) and place its new order (N – D) days after the delivery of the previous order. For a time period of 1 year,
   $N = 365/(S/Q*)$
7. If usage and/or lead time are not constant or known with certainty, then a safety stock of inventory must be carried. Its size depends on
   a. the degree of uncertainty associated with forecasted demand,
   b. the size and uncertainty of the lead time,
   c. the cost of being out of stock, in terms of both present and future sales,
   d. the cost of carrying inventory.
8. Recently in certain industries, computerization has made "just in time" inventory control possible: inventories are acquired at the exact times they are needed. This requires:
   a. a very accurate production and inventory information system,
   b. highly efficient purchasing,
   c. very reliable suppliers,
   d. an efficient inventory-handling system.

IV. Although inventory management is not the direct operating responsibility of the financial manager, the investment of funds in inventory is an important aspect of financial management.

APPENDIX:

Discriminant analysis is a statistical tool which can be used in the evaluation of the creditworthiness of a potential customer.

1. Start with a sample of historical credit customers, some which became bad accounts, and some which remained good.
2. Collect data on variables which might have predicted the creditworthiness of these customers.
3. Find the boundary line (discriminant function) that discriminates best between good and bad accounts:

$F_i = a_1X_{1i} + a_2X_{2i} + \ldots$, where,

f_i = calculated discriminant value for account i,

a_j = weight of the jth variable, obtained statistically,

X_{ji} = value of the jth variable for account i.

4. If the appropriate X variables were chosen, almost all good accounts should fall on one side of the line and bad accounts on the other. (There is no limit on the number of X variables that can be included in the discriminant function.)
5. Calculation of the F_i for each of the accounts should result in two probability distributions, one for the bad accounts and one for the good ones. These distributions may overlap slightly, but their means should be significantly far apart.
6. Using the weights obtained from the analysis, the financial manager can calculate F_i for a new account (given the account's X values), compare it to the F_is of the good and bad accounts, and calculate the probability that the new account will fall into one group or the other.

MULTIPLE CHOICE QUESTIONS

16.1 Relaxing credit standards will result in all except
a. increased sales.
b. higher opportunity costs.
c. lower bad debt expenses.
d. higher credit related costs.

16.2 CCC Company relaxes its credit standards and finds that its accounts receivable have increased by $100,000. Its variable cost is normally 60 percent of sales and the firm has substantial excess capacity. The firm has an opportunity to invest in marketable securities at a rate of 10 percent. Its opportunity cost in receivables from relaxing the credit standards is
a. $5,000.
b. $6,000.
c. $8,000.
d. $10,000.

16.3 If a company changes its terms of trade from 1/10, net 30 to 1/10, net 60, which of the following will not happen?
a. Sales will increase.
b. The old customers will continue to pay in 30 days.
c. The new customers will pay in 60 days.
d. Total receivables will increase.

16.4 For most credit-related policy variables, as the policy is varied from no effort to an extreme effort, profits _____ at an _____ rate up to a point.
a. increase, decreasing
b. increase, increasing
c. decrease, decreasing
d. decrease, increasing

16.5 The four C's of credit include all but the following:
a. collateral.
b. character.
c. cash.
d. capital.

16.6 The statistical technique used to assign applicants into "good" or "bad" credit risk classes is called
a. regression analysis.
b. good/bad assignment analysis.
c. numerical rating analysis.
d. discriminant analysis.

16.7 Inventory management involves a trade-off between
a. cost and production.
b. cost and flexibility.
c. timing and production.
d. materials and flexibility.

16.8 The DDD Company anticipates selling 100,000 units of its product evenly throughout the year. It costs $2 per unit to carry a unit in inventory for the year. Placing an order costs approximately $25. The company plans to carry 3,000 units in its safety stock. The economic order quantity is
a. 1,581.
b. 2,500.
c. 3,749.
d. 5,000.

16.9 The order point is the sum of
a. the safety stock and the order quantity.
b. the EOQ and the product of the usage rate and the lead time.
c. the safety stock and the average inventory.
d. the safety stock and the product of the usage rate and the lead time.

16.10 The average inventory is
    a. the EOQ.
    b. the EOQ plus the safety stock.
    c. the safety stock plus half the EOQ.
    d. the EOQ plus half of the safety stock.

ANSWERS

16.1 c p.   420
16.2 b p.   421 $(\$100,000)(0.6)(0.1) = \$6,000$

16.3 b pp. 423-424
16.4 a p.   427
16.5 c p.   431
16.6 d p.   431
16.7 b pp. 437-438
16.8 a p.   439 $$Q^* = [(2)(100,000)(25)/2]^{1/2}$$
                         $$= (2,500,000)^{1/2}$$
                         $$= 1,581$$

16.9 d pp. 441-442
16.10 c p.   443

CHAPTER 17

UNSECURED SHORT-TERM FINANCING

PERSPECTIVE

The financial manager can "package" debt instruments to take advantage of imperfections and incompleteness in financial markets. An important element in the package is maturity. Short-term debt is cheaper than long-term debt, but it is more risky. There are a number of alternative sources of short-term financing.

Trade credit is a readily available, flexible form of financing available from a company's suppliers. Accruals are a spontaneous, interest-free source of funds. Commercial paper can be used only by large, creditworthy corporations and is usually cheaper than the rates available on bank loans. Bankers' acceptance financing is usually associated with foreign trade transactions. Unsecured bank loans are available with a variety of conditions and costs.

CHAPTER OUTLINE

   I. Because imperfections and incompleteness exist in financial markets, stockholders benefit from the firm's altering the maturity, composition, and types of debt contracts employed.
      A. Fixed flotation costs create a bias toward less frequent financing, larger offerings of debt each time, and longer maturities.
      B. Bankruptcy costs create a bias in favor of longer maturities.
      C. If the cost of information is somewhat fixed to either the lender or the borrower, it creates a tendency toward less diversity in debt arrangements.
      D. Institutional constraints on lenders create a bias toward short- to intermediate-term loans.

  II. If a firm adopts a hedging approach to financing, the borrowing and payment schedule for short-term financing would be arranged to correspond to the expected swings in current assets.
      A. Fixed assets and the permanent component of current assets would be financed with long-term debt, equity, and the permanent component of current liabilities.
      B. Apart from current installments on long-term debt, a firm would show no current borrowings during seasons when it had surplus cash.

C. In a growth situation, permanent financing would be increased in keeping with underlying increases in permanent funds requirements.
D. An exact synchronization of the schedule of expected future net cash flows and the payment schedule of debt is not appropriate under conditions of uncertainty.
   1. Net cash flows will deviate from expected flows in keeping with the business risk of the firm.
   2. The shorter the maturity schedule of a firm's debt, the greater the risk that it will be unable to meet principal and interest payments.
   3. If a firm finances with short-term debt, it is uncertain of interest costs on refinancing, especially since short-term rates fluctuate more than long-term rates.
   4. A mitigating factor of financial risk is the possible covariance of short-term interest costs with operating income.
   5. The longer the maturity schedule of a firm's debt, the more costly the financing is likely to be over an extended period of time.

III. Trade credit is the largest source of short-term funds for business firms collectively.
   A. Because suppliers generally are more liberal in the extension of credit than are financial institutions, small companies in particular rely on trade credit.
   B. There are three types of trade credit.
      1. The open-account arrangement results from the shipment of goods accompanied by an invoice; no formal debt instrument is signed. This is by far the most common type of trade credit. There are varying terms of credit:
         a. Cash on delivery (COD) means that the seller does not extend credit, and the only risk borne is the shipping cost.
         b. Cash before delivery (CBD) means that the seller does not extend credit and is not willing to bear any risk at all.
         c. Progress payments, common in certain industries, require the buyer to pay the manufacturer at various stages of production prior to actual delivery of the finished product.
         d. Net period, no cash discount, is an extension of credit for a fixed time period, with no discount allowed for early payment.
         e. Net period with cash discount is an extension of credit for a fixed time period, with a discount allowed for early payment.
         f. Datings extend credit for a longer than normal period of time. Sellers frequently use seasonal datings to encourage customers to place their orders during slack seasons.

2. The seller may require that the buyer sign a promissory note which calls for payment at some specified future date.
3. Under a trade acceptance arrangement, the seller draws a time draft on the buyer, ordering the buyer to pay the draft at some date in the future. The seller will not release the goods until the buyer accepts the draft.

C. Trade credit is not necessarily a discretionary source of financing, but may depend entirely on the purchasing plans of the firm, which are dependent on its production cycle.

D. If a firm forgoes a cash discount and pays its bill on the final due date of the net period, there is an opportunity cost for the additional days. If the terms were 1/10, net 30, the annual cost would be
(1/99)(365/20) = 18.6%

E. The cost of trade credit decreases at a decreasing rate as the net period increases.

F. If a firm "stretches" accounts payable by postponing payment beyond the net period, it forgoes the cash discount and risks a possible deterioration in its credit rating. The seller may also increase prices to the buyer in the future.

G. The advantage over other forms of short-term financing is the absence of the need for formal negotiation; trade credit is readily available.

H. The supplier of a product for which demand is elastic may absorb most of the cost of trade credit; if demand is inelastic, he may pass the cost on to the buyer.

IV. Accrual accounts are the most spontaneous source of financing.
A. As sales increase, accrued wages increase; as profits increase, accrued taxes increase.

B. Accruals are an interest-free source of financing, but they are not discretionary; payment can only be postponed as a last resort by a company on the brink of a cash-flow disaster.

C. On a "one-shot" basis, a company can change the frequency of wage payments and thereby affect the amount of financing.

V. Large, well-established companies sometimes borrow through commercial paper and other money market instruments.
A. Commercial paper is an unsecured, negotiable promissory note sold in the money market and rated as to quality by Moody's, Standard & Poor's, and/or Fitch's.
1. The dealer market is composed of a half-dozen major dealers who purchase commercial paper from industrial firms, utilities, and medium-sized finance companies and resell it to investors.
a. The typical commission for a dealer is 1/8 percent.
b. Maturities generally range from 30 to 90 days.

        c. Paper generally has denominations of $100,000.
        d. Dealers require borrowers to maintain lines of credit in banks to assure that the paper can be paid off.
    2. Several large sales finance companies sell their paper directly to investors.
        a. Both maturity and the amount of the note are tailored to the needs of investors.
        b. Maturities can range from a few days to 270 days.
    3. Some corporations issue "bank-supported" commercial paper.
        a. A bank provides a letter of credit guaranteeing the investor that the company's obligation will be paid.
        b. The paper is rated on the creditworthiness of the bank.
        c. The bank usually charges a 1/8 or 1/4 percent commitment fee plus a 1/8 or 1/4 percent usage fee.

B. For a company engaged in foreign trade or the domestic storage and shipment of certain marketable goods, bankers' acceptances can be a major source of financing.
    1. Buyer and seller agree that a 90-day time draft will be used in settlement, and the American bank on which it is drawn accepts the draft.
    2. The bank substitutes its creditworthiness for the buyer's, and the draft (now a banker's acceptance) can be sold in the market at a discount.
    3. The borrower's interest rate is the discount rate plus fees to the bank and dealer, which frequently total 7/8 percent.

VI. Short-term, unsecured bank loans are usually regarded as self-liquidating because the assets purchased with the proceeds are supposed to generate sufficient cash flows to pay off the loan over time.
A. There are three types of unsecured bank loans.
    1. A line of credit is an arrangement between a bank and its customer, specifying the maximum amount of unsecured credit the bank will permit the firm to owe at any one time.
        a. Credit lines are usually established for a 1-year period and are subject to 1-year renewals.
        b. Because certain banks regard borrowing under lines of credit as seasonal or temporary financing, they may require that the company pay off the debt for a period of time during the year.
        c. While a bank has a moral obligation to honor a line of credit, it is not legally committed to do so.
    2. A revolving credit agreement is a legal commitment by the bank to extent credit up to a maximum amount.
        a. The borrower is usually required to pay a commitment fee on the unused portion of the credit.
        b. Agreements frequently extend beyond one year.

3. Transaction loans are separate arrangements made when the firm needs short-term funds for only one purpose, and the projected cash-flow ability of the borrower to repay the loan is the determining factor.

B. Expert systems have been developed for use by banks in making business loans, freeing up lending officers for complex lending situations.

C. Interest rates on most business loans are determined through personal negotiation between the borrower and the bank.
1. Interest rates vary with the creditworthiness of the borrower and with money market conditions.
2. The prime rate is a benchmark rate that changes with underlying market conditions.
3. A borrower may be charged the prime rate, or a rate higher or lower than the prime rate, depending on
   a. the borrower's creditworthiness,
   b. balances maintained and other business the borrower has with the bank,
   c. the cost of servicing the loan,
   d. competitive conditions in the local banking market,
   e. expected future business between the bank and the borrower.
4. Interest rates on small loans are generally higher than the rates on large loans.
5. Interest may be computed in several ways:
   a. on a collect basis, which means interest is paid at the maturity of the note and the nominal and effective rates are the same.
   b. on a discount basis, which means that interest is deducted from the initial loan and the effective rate is higher than the nominal rate.
   c. on an add-on basis for installment loans, which means that interest is added to the funds disbursed in order to determine the face value of the note and the periodic payments; the effective rate is approximately double the nominal rate.
6. Commercial banks often require the borrower to maintain a compensating balance, which is a demand-deposit balance whose minimum is a percentage of either the amount of funds borrowed or the amount of the commitment.
7. To the extent that the compensating balance required is larger than the balance the company would normally maintain at the bank, the effective rate on the loan increases.

MULTIPLE CHOICE QUESTIONS

17.1 Small and medium-sizes firms may be forced out of public offerings and into financing through banks because of
a. bankruptcy costs.
b. transactions costs.
c. the cost of information.
d. restrictions on lenders.

17.2 Which of the following is not true of long-term debt?
a. It is less risky than short-term debt to the issuer.
b. It is generally less expensive than short-term debt.
c. Over a number of years, the firm is more certain of its cash payments than with short-term debt.
d. Its interest rate varies less than short-term debt.

17.3 Which of the following is not a type of trade credit?
a. open account
b. trade notes payable
c. trade acceptances
d. trade paper

17.4 If the terms are 3/10, net 40, the effective cost of foregoing the discount (using a 360-day year) is
a. 27.0 percent.
b. 27.8 percent.
c. 36.0 percent.
d. 37.1 percent.

17.5 The greatest advantage of trade credit is its
a. cost.
b. availability.
c. lender restrictions.
d. flexibility.

17.6 The cost associated with accruals is
a. high.
b. variable.
c. zero.
d. uncertain.

17.7 If a large, well-established firm needed $10,000,000 for 2 months, it would probably raise it through
a. commercial paper.
b. bank loans.
c. certificates of deposit.
d. trade credit.

17.8 The principal advantage of commercial paper is its
   a. flexibility.
   b. cost.
   c. risk.
   d. tie-in with commercial banks.

17.9 Which of the following requires a periodic cleanup?
   a. a line of credit
   b. a revolving credit agreement
   c. a transaction loan
   d. an installment loan

17.10 On a loan on which the interest is paid on a discount basis
   a. the borrower receives the face amount of the loan.
   b. the effective interest rate is equal to the stated interest rate.
   c. the borrower receives less than the face amount of the loan.
   d. the effective interest rate is less than the stated interest rate.

ANSWERS

17.1   c   p.   458
17.2   b   pp. 459-460
17.3   d   p.   462
17.4   d   p.   464 $(3/97)(360/30) = 0.371$, or 37.1%

17.5   b   p.   466
17.6   c   pp. 467-468
17.7   a   p.   468
17.8   b   pp. 468-469
17.9   a   p.   471
17.10 c   p.   474

CHAPTER 18

SECURED LOANS AND TERM FINANCING

███

PERSPECTIVE

The market value of collateral for a secured loan must be greater than the outstanding balance of the loan. The principal assets to secure business loans are accounts receivable and inventories.

Receivables may either be assigned to secure a loan or sold to a factor. There are many ways to secure a loan with inventories.

Intermediate-term financing may be unsecured, in the form of term loans and revolving credit commitments, or secured by the pledge of equipment.

Lenders who offer unsecured credit usually impose restrictions called protective covenants on the borrower. If the borrower defaults under any of the loan provisions, the lender may initiate immediate corrective measures or force bankruptcy.

CHAPTER OUTLINE

I. A secured loan gives the lender two sources of repayment: the cash-flow ability of the firm to service the debt and the collateral value of the security.
    A. Secured lending arrangements have implied costs and benefits.
        1. They are more costly to administer than unsecured loans and this incremental cost is passed on to the borrower in the form of fees and higher interest costs.
        2. They may reduce conflict between creditors and reduce monitoring, enforcement, and foreclosure costs.
    B. Lenders usually seek security with a market value significantly above the amount of the loan.
        1. In default, if the security is sold for an amount exceeding the principal and interest owed, the difference is remitted to the borrower.
        2. If the security is sold for less, the lender becomes a general creditor for the amount of the difference.
        3. The marketability, life, and riskiness (fluctuation in market value) determine the attractiveness of various types of collateral.
        4. Article 9 of the Uniform Commercial Code, which is in force in all states, governs the procedures under which a lender obtains a security interest in the collateral.

II. Accounts receivable are desirable security for a loan because they are liquid assets.
   A. A lender usually advances between 50 and 80 percent of the face value of receivables, depending on their quality.
      1. The amount of the loan fluctuates as new receivables replace the old.
      2. Many banks do not require compensating balances for receivables loans.
      3. A service fee of 1 to 3 percent is usually charged to cover bookkeeping and other administrative costs to the lender.
      4. The interest rate on the loan is usually 2 to 4 percent over the prime rate.
      5. A cleanup of the loan is not required.
      6. The borrower retains title to the receivables.
   B. The larger the size of receivables, the more desirable they are as collateral because the less it costs per dollar of loan to process them.
      1. A firm that sells low-priced items on open account will generally be unable to obtain a receivables loan.
      2. A floating or blanket assignment of receivables may be used to solve the small-account problem, but it makes preventing fraud difficult.
   C. A receivable loan can be on either a nonnotification or a notification basis.
      1. Under a nonnotification basis, the customer pays the borrower who forwards the check to the lender.
      2. Under a notification basis, remittance is made directly to the lender.
   D. When a firm factors its receivables, it sells them to a factor under an annually renewable contract.
      1. The factor maintains a credit department and buys only accounts which it considers to be acceptable credit risks.
      2. Most firms eliminate their own credit departments and will not sell on credit to customers whose accounts the factor will not buy.
      3. The sale may be with or without recourse, and on a notification or nonnotification basis, depending on the arrangement negotiated.
      4. The total cost of factoring is composed of a factoring fee plus an interest charge if the firm draws on its account before the receivables are collected.
      5. The factoring fee, or commission, varies with the size and quality of the accounts, and with the volume of receivables sold.

III. Inventory that is relatively standard, and for which a ready market exists, is also suitable security for loans.
   A. Lenders determine the percentage that they are willing to advance by considering the inventory's:

1. marketability,
2. perishability,
3. market price stability,
4. difficulty and expense to liquidate.
  B. There are three methods of making inventory loans that leave the inventory in the possession of the borrower.
    1. The lender can obtain a floating lien on all inventory of the borrower.
      a. The lien can be modified to cover both receivables and inventories.
      b. The lien can be modified to encompass future as well as present inventory.
    2. With a chattel mortgage, inventories are identified specifically by serial number or some other means, and cannot be sold unless the lender consents.
    3. With a trust receipt loan, inventories are identified specifically but the borrower is allowed to sell them; he must turn the proceeds of the sale over to the lender, who periodically audits the inventory.
  C. Inventory loans can be made on the basis of negotiable or nonnegotiable warehouse receipts, which are evidence that specified inventory has been put into the possession of a third party.
    1. A borrower secures a terminal warehouse receipt loan by storing inventory with a public warehouse.
    2. A field warehousing company sets off a designated storage area on the borrower's premises for the inventory pledged as collateral, has sole access to this area, and maintains strict control over it.
    3. Either type of warehouse can release the collateral to the borrower only when authorized to do so by the lender.

IV. There are various forms of intermediate-term debt, which generally matures in 1 to 5 years.
  A. Bank term loans have a maturity of more than one year and are usually repaid in equal periodic installments.
    1. There may occasionally be a balloon payment, a final payment which is larger than any of the others.
    2. The interest rate may be fixed or variable.
    3. Legal and commitment fees may also be charged.
    4. The terms and conditions of the loan are arranged through direct negotiation, and can be renegotiated if the firm's requirements change.
  B. Revolving credit commitments are usually for 3 years, although the actual notes evidencing debt are short term, usually 90 days.
    1. The bank is legally bound under the loan agreement to have funds available whenever the company wants to borrow, and usually requires a commitment fee as compensation.

2. Revolving credit agreements can be set up so that at the maturity of the commitment, the amount then owed can be converted into a term loan at the option of the borrower.

C. Insurance company term loans generally mature in more than 10 years, require a higher rate of interest, and contain prepayment penalties.

D. Equipment financing involves the pledging of specific equipment as collateral for a loan.
1. The repayment schedule for the loan is usually timed to the economic life of the equipment.
2. The lender wants to be sure that the market value of the equipment always exceeds the balance of the loan.
3. The interest charged by a finance company is usually higher than that charged by a commercial bank.
4. If the equipment loan is obtained from the equipment seller, the interest charge will depend on the extent to which the financing arrangement is seen as a sales tool.
5. Equipment loans may be secured by either:
   a. a chattel mortgage, or
   b. a conditional sales contract (the seller retains title until the purchaser has satisfied all the terms of the contract). This contract may be sold to a bank or finance company with recourse.

V. Restrictive covenants are provisions built into a loan agreement to protect the lender.
A. Failure to meet these provisions constitutes default just as much as failure to pay interest or repay principal.
B. Most loans contain covenants which place:
1. a floor under working capital,
2. a ceiling on cash dividends and repurchases of stock,
3. a ceiling on capital expenditures,
4. limitations on other indebtedness.
C. Routine mechanical restrictions
1. require the borrower to furnish financial statements at specified times,
2. require the borrower to maintain adequate insurance,
3. prohibit the sale of significant amounts of assets,
4. forbid the pledging or mortgaging of assets,
5. forbid the discounting or sale of receivables,
6. limit the amount of leasing,
7. prohibit mergers unless specifically approved by the lender.
D. Special provisions in specific loan agreements may
1. spell out the use of the loan proceeds,
2. limit nonliquid investments,
3. require key executive life insurance, payable to the lender to be applied to the loan,
4. prevent excessive compensation of executives.
E. Under a well-written loan agreement, a borrower cannot get into serious financial difficulty without defaulting under

a covenant, thereby giving the lender legal authority to take corrective action.

VI. The debtholder-equityholder relationship can be visualized as essentially an option arrangement.
   A. The face value of the debt can be thought of as the exercise price of an option.
      1. In default, the ownership of the firm passes to the debtholders who realize less than the contractual amount of their claim; the equityholders receive nothing.
      2. At maturity, the equityholders pay off the loan and receive the total remaining value of the firm.
   B. The value of an option increases with the variance of the value of the associated asset, in this case, the firm itself.
      1. Increasing the risk of the firm increases the variance of its total value and therefore transfers wealth from the debtholders to the equityholders.
      2. Protective covenants that will trigger default give the debtholders the ability to force bankruptcy and can therefore preclude equityholders from increasing the risk of the company.
      3. The restrictiveness of protective covenants is the result of negotiation between debtholders and equityholders, given relative conditions in the financial markets and the costs of monitoring the enforcement of the covenants.

MULTIPLE CHOICE QUESTIONS

18.1 Which of the following characteristics is not desirable for collateral?
   a. ready marketability
   b. special purpose
   c. stable market value
   d. cash-flow life parallels the life of the loan

18.2 A blanket assignment of receivables is an attempt to alleviate the problem of
   a. obsolete inventories.
   b. fraud.
   c. uncreditworthy customers.
   d. many small accounts receivable.

18.3 The net cost of factoring can be reduced because of
   a. interest charged on funds advanced.
   b. the factoring commission on the receivables factored.
   c. the elimination of the credit and collection departments.
   d. the reserve the factor maintains for disputed items.

18.4 Trust receipt loans are more likely to be used by
  a. drug stores.
  b. department stores.
  c. farm equipment dealers.
  d. clothing stores.

18.5 Which of the following is not related to using inventories as security for a loan?
  a. chattel mortgage
  b. trust receipt loan
  c. warehouse receipt loan
  d. factoring

18.6 A loan in which the inventory is kept on the borrower's premises but is separated from other inventory and is controlled by an outsider is called a
  a. terminal warehouse receipt loan.
  b. trust receipt loan.
  c. field warehouse receipt loan.
  d. chattel mortgage loan.

18.7 Intermediate-term debt generally refers to debt with a maturity of from _____ to _____.
  a. 1 month, 5 years
  b. 1 year, 5 years
  c. 3 years, 5 years
  d. 5 years, 10 years

18.8 Which of the following is not an example of intermediate-term lending?
  a. factoring
  b. bank term loans
  c. insurance company term loans
  d. equipment financing

18.9 Restrictive covenants protect
  a. lenders.
  b. borrowers.
  c. stockholders.
  d. management.

18.10 We would expect that the greater the number of protective covenants in a loan provision, the
  a. greater the interest rate.
  b. lower the monitoring costs.
  c. happier the management of the borrowing firm.
  d. lower the interest rate.

ANSWERS

18.1	b	pp.	481-482
18.2	d	p.	483
18.3	c	p.	484
18.4	c	p.	486
18.5	d	p.	486

18.6	c	p.	488
18.7	b	p.	489
18.8	a	pp.	489-490
18.9	a	pp.	492-493
18.10	d	p.	494

████████████████████████████████

PERSPECTIVE

In lease financing, the lessee agrees to pay the lessor, periodically, for use of the lessor's asset. Because this is a contractual obligation, leasing is a method of financing similar to borrowing. It can be direct, leveraged, or involve a sale and leaseback.

Accounting procedures distinguish between capital leases and operating leases. Financial evaluation of leases may use either the net present value or the internal rate of return methods, but the decision to employ lease or debt financing occurs only after investment in the asset has been judged acceptable.

Imperfections in the capital markets such as bankruptcy costs and differences in taxation permit the use of lease financing to increase shareholder wealth.

CHAPTER OUTLINE

I. A lease is a contract whereby the owner of an asset (the lessor) grants to another (the lessee) the exclusive right to use the asset, usually for an agreed period of time, in return for the payment of rent.
   A. In exchange for the use of an asset without having to buy it, the lessee makes periodic lease payments, usually monthly or quarterly and in advance.
   B. Lease contracts can have various terms.
      1. Under a maintenance lease, the lessor pays for maintenance, repairs, taxes, and insurance; under a net lease, the lessee pays these costs.
      2. A lease may be cancelable (with or without a penalty) or noncancelable.
      3. An operating lease is for a period shorter than the asset's economic life, and is cancelable with proper notice; a financial lease lasts as long as the asset and is noncancelable.
      4. At expiration, the lessee may or may not have the right to renew the lease (at the same or a different rent), and/or to purchase the asset for fair market value.
   C. There are three major types of lease financing.
      1. Under a sale and leaseback arrangement, a firm sells an asset at approximately its market value to another party, who then leases it back to the firm.

a. The lessee receives the sales price in cash and use of the asset during the lease period.

b. The lessor receives periodic payments, title to the asset, and any residual value at the end of the lease.

c. If the asset involves land the lessee improves its tax position because lease payments are tax deductible but land is not depreciable.

d. Insurance companies, other institutional investors, finance companies, and independent leasing companies tend to engage in sale and leasebacks.

2. Under direct leasing, a company acquires the use of an asset it did not own previously.

a. The lessor may or may not be the manufacturer.

b. In certain cases, a lessor may achieve economies of scale in the purchase of capital assets and may pass them on to the lessee in the form of lower lease payments.

3. Under leveraged leasing, there are three parties involved: the lessee, the lessor (or equity participant), and the lender.

a. For the lessee, there is no difference between a leveraged lease and any other type of lease.

b. The lessor acquires the asset by borrowing most of the cost and assigning the lease and lease payments while retaining the right to deduct depreciation and retain salvage value.

c. The lender usually holds a mortgage on the asset.

II. The accounting treatment of leases was changed in 1976.

A. FASB13 requires capitalization on the balance sheet of leases which meet any one of the following conditions:

1. The lease transfers title to the asset to the lessee by the end of the lease period.

2. The lease contains an option to purchase the asset at a bargain price.

3. The lease period is equal to, or greater than, 75 percent of the estimated economic life of the asset.

4. At the beginning of the lease, the present value of the minimum lease payments equals or exceeds 90 percent of the fair value of the asset.

B. The lessee must report the value of the leased property as an asset.

1. The amount of the asset is the present value of the minimum lease payments over the lease period.

2. If executory costs, such as insurance, maintenance, and taxes, are part of the total lease payment, these are deducted before calculating present value.

3. The discount rate is the lower of either:

a. the lessee's incremental borrowing rate, or

b. the lessor's implicit interest rate.

4. If the fair market value of the leased property is lower than the present value of the minimum lease payments, then the fair market value is shown on the balance sheet.
5. The present value of lease payments due within 1 year is a current liability to the lessee, and the present value of payments due after 1 year is a noncurrent liability.
6. A capital lease must be amortized by the lessee's usual depreciation method, over the term of the lease.
7. Both the amortization of leased property and the annual interest embodied in the lease payment are treated as an expense on the lessee's income statement.
   C. Operating leases can be reported in footnotes to the balance sheet, and the lease payment itself is deductible as an expense on the income statement.

III. The treatment of capital leases for tax purposes differs from their treatment for accounting purposes.
   A. The IRS has defined criteria to ensure that a lease is not a disguised installment purchase of the asset.
      1. The term of the lease cannot exceed 90 percent of the useful life of the asset.
      2. If the lessee has any options at the end of the lease, they must be based on the fair market value of the asset.
      3. The lease payments must provide the lessor not only a return of principal but a reasonable interest return as well.
      4. The lease term must be less than 30 years.
   B. For tax purposes, the annual lease payment is deductible as an expense if the above criteria are met.

IV. Once a decision is reached to acquire an asset, the firm must decide how it is to be financed.
   A. The before-tax return to the lessor can be found by solving the following equation for R:

$$V = \sum_{t=0}^{n} L/(1 + R)^t, \text{ where,}$$

   V = cost of the asset now,
   L = annual lease payment, with the first payment being made now.
   B. The relevant comparison for the lessee is the cost of debt financing versus the cost of lease financing.
      1. According to the present value method, whichever alternative has the lower present value is the most desirable.
         a. If the asset is leased, the lease payments in time t and their corresponding tax savings in time t+1 are discounted at the after-tax cost of borrowing.
         b. If the asset is purchased, the cash flows that are discounted at the after-tax cost of borrowing are:

126

the loan payment
less the tax shield on the interest,
plus the after-tax maintenance costs (if any),
less the tax shield on the depreciation,
plus the after-tax residual value.
2. Instead of computing the present values, one could compute the internal rates of return and choose whichever alternative has the higher IRR.
   a. The after-tax cost of leasing can be found by solving the following equation for r:

$$A_0 = \sum_{t=0}^{n-1} L_t/(1 + r)^t + \sum_{t=1}^{n} [T(L_{t-1} - P_t)/(1 + r)^t]$$
$$- RV(1 - T)/(1 + r)^n, \text{ where,}$$

   A_0 = cost of the asset to be leased,
   n = number of periods to the end of the lease,
   L_t = lease payment at end of period t,
   T = corporate tax rate,
   P_t = depreciation in period t,
   RV = expected residual value at end of lease.
   b. If the asset is purchased, the same cash flows are used as for present value.
C. If a floating-rate is used rather than a fixed rate, most analysts employ either the present short-term borrowing rate or some average of expected future short-term borrowing rates.
D. When borrowing costs are uncertain, sensitivity analysis may be used to determine how much and how fast the borrowing rate must change before one is indifferent between lease and debt financing.
E. If an asset can be leased but not purchased, the only decision is whether or not to lease.
   1. Determine the cash-equivalent price of the lease alternative, which is the present value of all required lease payments discounted by an interest rate that is consistent with other current leasing arrangements.
   2. Compute the present value of expected future cash benefits associated with the project over the lease period, discounted at the required rate of return.
   3. If the present value of the expected future cash benefits exceeds the cash-equivalent price, the project should be accepted; if not, it should be rejected.

V. Leasing is a thing of value because the capital markets are imperfect and incomplete.
   A. If the capital markets were complete and perfect, the costs of debt and lease financing would be the same.
   B. The two market imperfections that have a systematic and predictable impact on the value of leasing are bankruptcy costs and taxes.
      1. In bankruptcy, the lessor's position is superior to that of a supplier of capital.

a. The lessor owns the asset and can retrieve it when the lessee defaults.

b. Neither the out-of-pocket costs nor the delays of bankruptcy affect the lessor as much as the secured lender.

2. Companies, financial institutions, and individuals derive different tax benefits from owning assets, so the lessor may obtain tax benefits from ownership and pass part of them on to the lessee.

a. Different tax rates apply to various individuals and corporations.

b. Different levels of past and current taxable income exist among various individuals and corporations.

c. The presence of the alternative minimum tax causes divergences in the ability of different corporations and individuals to use fully accelerated depreciation and the deduction of interest as an expense.

C. Tax considerations are important in deciding whether to lease or borrow.

1. The exact sharing of tax benefits between lessor and lessee is negotiable.

2. The benefits are reflected in the amount of the periodic lease payments relative to the cost of the asset involved, or in the implied interest cost of the lease.

3. In the U.S., many companies that have relatively low profitability lease large, expensive assets such as airplanes, ships, railroad cars, computers, and machinery to obtain a significant portion of the tax benefits they would otherwise be unable to realize.

D. There may be other reasons for the advantages of lease financing.

1. The lessor may enjoy economies of scale in the purchase of assets that are not available to the lessee.

2. The lessor may have a different estimate of the life of the asset, its salvage value, or the discount rate, than the lessee.

3. The lessor may face lower borrowing costs than the lessee.

4. The lessor may be able to provide expertise to its customers in equipment selection and maintenance.

MULTIPLE CHOICE QUESTIONS

19.1 A lease that is relatively short-term and is cancelable with proper notice is a
a. capital lease.
b. operating lease.
c. leveraged lease.
d. sale and leaseback.

19.2　A financial lease is
　　　a. short-term.
　　　b. cancelable.
　　　c. one whose life approximates the life of the asset.
　　　d. typical of the leases on copiers.

19.3　In a leveraged lease, the residual value goes to the
　　　a. lessor.
　　　b. lessee.
　　　c. lender.
　　　d. government.

19.4　In a leveraged lease, the lessor is also a
　　　a. lender.
　　　b. borrower.
　　　c. manufacturer.
　　　d. low-taxed firm.

19.5　If a lease gives the lessee the right to buy the asset at the
　　　end of the lease for $1, the lease is a
　　　a. capital lease.
　　　b. operating lease.
　　　c. leveraged lease.
　　　d. sale and leaseback.

19.6　The accounting treatment for a capital lease is to show
　　　a. the asset on the books.
　　　b. the liability on the books.
　　　c. both the asset and the liability on the books.
　　　d. the details in the footnotes to the financial statements.

19.7　A manufacturer's representative suggests to you that your
　　　firm should lease a new machine that he says is the latest
　　　thing on the market.　Which of the following should you do
　　　first?
　　　a. determine the leasing cash flows
　　　b. determine the depreciation schedule
　　　c. determine the interest payments on a loan that could be
　　　　 obtained to finance the asset
　　　d. determine if acquiring the asset has a positive NPV

19.8　For an asset whose use can only be acquired through leasing,
　　　a. the analysis is solely an investment decision.
　　　b. the analysis is purely a financial decision.
　　　c. the decision is a choice between leasing and borrowing.
　　　d. the investment and financing decisions are intertwined.

19.9　The most important reason for the existence of leasing is
　　　a. bankruptcy costs.
　　　b. corporate taxes.
　　　c. personal taxes.
　　　d. differences in tax rates.

19.10 In analyzing the lease versus borrow decision, the most
uncertain cash flow is most likely the
a. depreciation tax shield.
b. lease payment tax shield.
c. residual value.
d. cost of the asset.

ANSWERS

19.1	b	p. 503		19.6	c	p.	506
19.2	c	p. 503		19.7	d	p.	508
19.3	a	p. 505		19.8	d	pp.	514-515
19.4	b	p. 505		19.9	d	p.	517
19.5	a	p. 506		19.10	c	p.	512

CHAPTER 20

CHANGING FINANCIAL MARKETS

PERSPECTIVE

The purpose of financial markets is the efficient allocation of savings to ultimate users of funds. Financial intermediaries transform the direct claims of ultimate borrowers into indirect claims, which are sold to ultimate lenders. When intermediation becomes inefficient it is reversed by securitization or by other means.

Inflation causes the real return on a security to be less than its nominal return. The Fisher effect suggests that the nominal return equals the sum of the real rate of interest plus the rate of inflation. Theoretical models question the equality of the relationship and empirical studies indicate that the relationship is not consistent over time.

Unanticipated changes in inflation also impact contractual relationships within the company, such as debtor-creditor claims, depreciation tax shields, inventory profits, price and cost sensitivities, and pension plans; stock valuation also may change.

Financial innovations are a response to profit-making opportunities that arise because changes in the economic environment make existing markets less perfect and/or incomplete.

CHAPTER OUTLINE

I. The purpose of financial markets in an economy is to allocate savings efficiently to ultimate users.
   A. In modern economies, the economic units which are savers are not the same as the economic units which invest.
      1. Households have total savings in excess of total investment.
      2. Nonfinancial corporations use more than their total savings for investing in real assets.
   B. Financial intermediaries facilitate the flow of savings from savers to users of funds by transforming direct claims into indirect ones.
      1. Financial intermediaries include institutions such as commercial banks, life insurance companies, and pension and profit-sharing funds.
      2. Financial intermediaries purchase primary securities (debt and equity instruments) on more attractive terms than would be available directly from savers, and issue their own securities (deposit accounts, insurance

131

policies, and so forth) which are well suited to the small saver.
3. Financial intermediaries provide many services.
   a. Transactions costs and costs associated with locating potential borrowers and savers are lowered because of economies of scale.
   b. Reliable information on the ultimate borrower can be developed efficiently, and confidential information can be protected.
   c. They can offer and purchase securities of varying denomination and can offer flexible terms to a large number of small lenders.
   d. Through adequate diversification, they can reduce risk.
   e. They can offer and purchase securities of varying maturities.
   f. They are expert in purchasing primary securities and in offering indirect securities, eliminating inconvenience for both saver and user.
C. Disintermediation occurs when the intermediation process becomes cumbersome and too costly; there is a reversion toward direct loans and security issues.
   1. Securitization involves packaging a pool of like illiquid assets and issuing securities backed by the package, giving the investor a direct claim on a portion of the pool.
   2. The total transaction costs of credit often are less with securitization than they are when a depository institution intermediates between borrowers and savers.
D. There are four main sectors in an economy.
   1. Households, whose assets are more financial than real, and whose net worth far exceeds their financial liabilities.
   2. Businesses, whose assets are more real than financial, and whose net worth exceeds their financial liabilities.
   3. Governments, whose assets are more real than financial, and whose financial liabilities far exceed their net worth.
   4. Financial intermediaries, whose assets are predominantly financial, and whose financial liabilities far exceed their net worth.
E. The more developed the financial markets, the greater the choices of the saver and the greater the financing opportunities available to the borrower, resulting in a higher level of capital formation, growth, and want satisfaction.

II. The allocation of funds in an economy occurs primarily on the basis of price, expressed in terms of expected return.
A. Except for inefficiencies caused by capital rationing, government restrictions, and institutional constraints,

savings will tend to be allocated to the most efficient uses.
   1. If risk is held constant, economic units willing to pay the highest expected return are the ones entitled to the use of funds.
   2. If rationality prevails, the economic units offering the highest returns will be the ones with the most promising investment opportunities.
   B. In market equilibrium, if all financial instruments had exactly the same risk characteristics, they would provide the same expected return.
   C. In reality, different financial instruments have different degrees of risk, caused by differences in:
   1. default risk,
   2. maturity,
   3. the level of coupon rate,
   4. taxation of interest, dividend, and capital gains returns,
   5. option-type features.
   D. The expected return on any financial instrument depends on the real rate of interest in the economy and on expected inflation.

III. The real rate of return on a security is less than the nominal rate of return.
   A. The expected return to a supplier of capital is the rate of discount that equates the present value of the stream of expected cash inflows with the purchase price.
   1. The expected return is expressed in nominal terms because the cash inflows received are in current dollars at the time of receipt.
   2. With inflation, these dollars will be worth less in purchasing power than were the dollars put out at the time the security was bought.
   3. The real return is the rate realized when all cash flows are placed on the same purchasing-power basis.
   B. The Fisher effect states that the nominal rate of interest embodies in it an inflation premium sufficient to compensate lenders for the expected loss of purchasing power associated with the receipt of future dollars.
   1. The Fisher effect can be formulated as
      $1 + r = (1 + R)(1 + \alpha)$, where,
         r = the nominal rate,
         R = the real rate,
         α = the inflation rate.
   2. When the rate of inflation is small or moderate,
      $r = R + \alpha$.
   3. The Fisher effect implies that if expected inflation rises by 1 percent, the nominal interest rate will also rise by 1 percent.
   C. Different economic theories exist to explain why the change in rates should not be equal.

133

1. Because inflation reduces real money balances, the nominal rate of interest will rise by less than the rise in expected inflation.
2. Because of taxes, the nominal rate of interest will rise by more than the rise in expected inflation.
D. Empirical studies indicate that the relationship is not consistent over time.
1. Studies based on data for the 1960s and 1970s suggest a less than one-to-one relationship between changes in nominal rates of interest and changes in inflation.
2. Later studies suggest either a one-to-one or greater than one-to-one relationship.

IV. Unanticipated changes in inflation affect contracts specified in nominal terms.
A. Whenever an unanticipated change in inflation occurs, the lender does not receive the real return expected at the time the loan was made.
1. An unanticipated increase in inflation benefits the borrower because the loan is repaid with cheaper dollars than originally anticipated.
2. An unanticipated decrease in inflation benefits the lender because the loan is repaid with more expensive dollars than originally anticipated.
3. Net creditors are economic units whose financial assets exceed their financial liabilities; the household sector and financial institutions are net creditors.
4. Net debtors are economic units whose financial liabilities exceed their financial assets; businesses and governments are net debtor sectors.
5. Unanticipated increases in inflation transfer real wealth from net creditors to net debtors.
6. Unanticipated decreases in inflation transfer real wealth from net debtors to net creditors.
B. Wages, materials costs, and product prices may respond to an unanticipated change in inflation and, therefore, change a firm's value.
1. When prices, wages, and other costs vary proportionately with unanticipated changes in inflation, the firm's value should rise so that the real return on capital is roughly unchanged.
2. If prices rise more rapidly than wages and other costs, the firm's value should increase.
3. If prices rise more slowly than wages and other costs, the firm's value should fall.
C. Unanticipated changes in inflation can also affect a firm's value because of the contractual nature of depreciation, inventories, and pension plan contributions.
1. Because a company is able to deduct only historical cost depreciation and not replacement cost depreciation, its real rate of return falls when prices rise, depressing share prices.

134

2. Inventories recorded on the first-in, first-out (FIFO) basis tend to cause accounting profits to be overstated and after-tax profits to be reduced when prices rise; this lowers the real rate of return and depresses share prices.
3. Unanticipated changes in inflation have an impact on a firm's pension plan and its explicit as well as implicit obligations to existing and future employees.

D. The theory that increasing inflation and rising interest rates cause stockholders to suffer a money illusion and value the stock lower than its true value is controversial.

V. The last 15 years have been characterized by tremendous financial innovation.
A. A new financial product or process will be profitable only if it makes the market more efficient and/or complete.
1. A financial innovation may make the market more efficient by reducing the spread between what the ultimate saver receives for funds and what the ultimate borrower pays, holding risk constant, or by lowering transaction and inconvenience costs.
2. If the market is incomplete, a firm or financial institution can make a profit and lower financing costs by tailoring security offerings to the unsatisfied desires of investors.
B. In an unchanging world, the market should be both efficient and complete.
C. The last 15 years have been characterized by:
1. changes in tax laws,
2. technological advances,
3. changes in the levels and volatilities of inflation, interest rates, and international currency values,
4. changes in the level of economic activity,
5. regulatory change.
D. Any one of these factors is sufficient to upset the equilibrium, create profit opportunities, and result in new financial products and processes.

MULTIPLE CHOICE QUESTIONS

20.1 Financial institutions assist individuals by doing all of the following except
a. lowering transactions costs.
b. reducing risk.
c. providing expertise and convenience.
d. allowing borrowing and lending at the same rate.

20.2 The process that takes an illiquid asset and transforms it into a security is called
a. intermediation.
b. disintermediation.
c. securitization.
d. financialization.

20.3 The major class of assets held by financial institutions is
a. land.
b. other real assets.
c. financial assets.
d. cash.

20.4 Funds are allocated in the U.S. economy primarily on the basis of
a. price.
b. government planning.
c. institutional constraints.
d. capital rationing.

20.5 The difference between the nominal rate and the real rate is a premium due to
a. risk.
b. expected inflation.
c. unanticipated inflation.
d. maturity.

20.6 An investment is expected to generate a 12 percent return, ignoring inflation. If the expected rate of inflation over the life of the asset is 3 percent, the _____ return is _____ percent.
a. nominal, 15
b. real, 15
c. real, 12
d. real, 9

20.7 According to the Fisher effect, if expected inflation increases by 2 percent, the nominal rate should
a. stay the same.
b. increase by less than 2 percent.
c. increase by 2 percent.
d. increase by more than 2 percent.

20.8 If actual inflation is less than anticipated,
a. lenders gain and borrowers lose.
b. borrowers gain and lenders lose.
c. both borrowers and lenders gain.
d. both borrowers and lenders lose.

20.9 Which of the following statements is true?
   a. Households and governments are net creditors.
   b. Households and businesses are net creditors.
   c. Businesses and governments are net debtors.
   d. Businesses and households are net debtors.

20.10 Financial innovation has been the result of all except
   a. tax changes.
   b. increased regulation.
   c. volatile inflation and interest rates.
   d. technological advances.

ANSWERS

20.1	d	pp.	527-528
20.2	c	pp.	528-529
20.3	c	p.	529
20.4	a	p.	530
20.5	b	p.	531

20.6	d	p.	531
20.7	c	p.	531
20.8	a	p.	534
20.9	c	pp.	534-535
20.10	b	p.	538

CHAPTER 21

ISSUING SECURITIES

PERSPECTIVE

When companies need to raise funds by selling securities to the public, they use the services of an investment banker. Its principal functions are risk bearing, or underwriting, and selling the securities. Its compensation is the spread between the price paid for the securities and the price at which they are resold.

A company may issue new common stock to the public or offer it to its existing shareholders on a privileged subscription basis. A right represents an option to buy the new security at the subscription price, and usually has a market value.

The SEC is the regulatory authority overseeing the sale of new securities and the trading of existing securities in the secondary market.

Venture capitalists specialize in financing new enterprises, accepting large probabilities of total loss in exchange for infrequent, huge returns. These returns are realized when the company makes its initial public offering of common stock.

The announcement of a new security issue may be accompanied by a stock market reaction because of asymmetric information between investors and management. Investors presume management will finance with stock when it believes the stock is overvalued and with debt when the stock is believed to be undervalued.

CHAPTER OUTLINE

I. An investment banking firm is a financial institution which acts as middleman in the distribution of new securities to the public.
   A. The difference between the price it pays the company for the security and the price at which the securities are resold to the public is called the spread.
      1. Investment banking firms have the expertise, the contacts, and the sales organization necessary to efficiently market securities to investors.
      2. Investment bankers can distribute securities at a lower cost than the issuing firm.
      3. The investment banker underwrites the sale of the issue by giving the company a check for the purchase price.
         a. If the issue does not sell well, either because of an adverse turn in the market or because it is overpriced, the underwriter takes the loss.

b. To spread risk and obtain better distribution, it invites other investment bankers to form a syndicate to participate in the offering.

c. The originating house usually is the manager and has the largest participation.

d. Each member of the syndicate is liable for its percentage participation in the unsold securities of the syndicate, regardless of the number of securities the individual member sells.

e. After the issue is sold, the spread less expenses and managing fee, is distributed to the members of the syndicate on the basis of their percentage participation.

4. A traditional underwriting can originate in either of two ways.

a. The issuing company can ask for competitive bids from interested syndicates, and the highest bid submitted at the specified time and place wins the security.

b. Negotiations initiated directly by either the issuing firm or the investment banker determine the essential features of the issue, as well as its price and timing.

5. An underwriter will occasionally make a market for a security after it is issued, which means that it:

a. maintains a position in the security,

b. quotes bid and asked prices,

c. stands ready to buy and sell at those prices.

B. If investment bankers are unwilling to accept the risk that a security will not sell, they may arrange to sell the issue on a best efforts basis.

1. They do not buy the issue themselves.

2. They agree only to sell as many securities as they can at an established price.

3. They bear no responsibility for securities that are unsold.

C. Often 2 or more months elapse between the time a company decides to finance and the time a security offering actually takes place.

1. Registering the issue with the Securities and Exchange Commission (SEC) accounts for several weeks.

a. A detailed registration statement and a prospectus must be submitted to the SEC.

b. The SEC reviews these documents to protect investors from misinformation and fraud.

c. Any deficiencies must be corrected before the security can be sold.

2. Rule 415 permits a shelf registration, which means that the company can register a large block of securities (enough for the next 2 years) at once, and can, from time to time, auction off some of them after filing a brief amendment to its original registration report.

3. Shelf registrations allow a company to go to market with a new issue in a matter of days, and cut the underwriting spread approximately in half.
4. Smaller corporations do not use shelf registrations.

D. The federal government regulates the sale of securities to the public.
   1. The Securities Act of 1933 requires full disclosure of information on the sale of new securities to investors.
   2. The Securities Exchange Act of 1934 regulates securities already outstanding; it created the SEC to enforce the two acts.
   3. The SEC is not concerned with the investment value of securities being issued, only with the presentation of complete and accurate information on all material facts regarding the securities.
   4. The SEC also regulates the sale of securities in the secondary markets.
      a. It regulates the activities of the securities exchanges, the over-the-counter market, investment bankers and brokers, the National Association of Securities Dealers, and investment companies.
      b. It requires monthly reports on stock transactions by officers, directors, and large stockholders ("insider trading").
      c. It requires the filing of form 13D whenever an investor or group obtains 5 percent or more of the outstanding stock of a company.
      d. It attempts to prevent manipulative practices, fraud, and misrepresentative promotion.

E. Individual states have security commissions that regulate the issuance of new securities in their states.
   1. State laws attempt to prevent the false promotion and sale of securities ("blue-sky laws").
   2. State laws are important when a security issue is sold entirely to people within the state and when a security issue is less than $1.5 million.
   3. State laws vary greatly in their effectiveness.

II. Instead of selling stock to new investors, a company can offer shares to existing shareholders on a privileged subscription basis.
    A. Unless a company's charter denies shareholders a preemptive right, they must be given the right to subscribe to new stock so that they maintain their proportionate interest in the company.
    B. When a company makes a rights offering, it mails its stockholders one right for each share of stock held.
       1. The terms of the offering specify the number of rights required to subscribe to an additional share of stock, the subscription price per share, and the expiration date of the offering.

2. The holder of rights has three choices:
   a. to exercise the rights and subscribe for additional shares,
   b. to sell the rights,
   c. to do nothing and let them expire.
C. Stock sells ex-rights after the date of record; an investor who buys the stock after this date does not receive the right to subscribe to additional stock.
   1. The theoretical market value of one right, while the stock is still selling rights-on, is
      $R_0 = (P_0 - S)/(N + 1)$, where,
         P_0 = market value of a share selling rights-on,
         S = subscription price per share,
         N = number of rights required to purchase one share.
   2. The theoretical value of one share of stock when it goes ex-rights is
      $P_x = [(P_0)(N) + S]/(N + 1)$.
   3. The theoretical value of a right when the stock sells ex-rights is
      $R_x = (P_x - S)/N$.
   4. The actual value of a right may differ from its theoretical value because of transaction costs, speculation, and the irregular exercise and sale of rights over the subscription period, but arbitrage limits the difference.
D. If the market price of the stock should fall below the subscription price, stockholders will not subscribe to the stock.
   1. The risk that the market price will fall below the subscription price is inversely related to N.
   2. The risk that the market price will fall below the subscription price is also a function of the volatility of the company's stock, the tone of the market, earnings expectations, and other factors.
   3. The greater the discount from the current market price, the greater the value of the right, and the greater the probability of a successful sale of stock.
   4. But the greater the discount, the more shares that will have to be issued to raise a given amount of money, and the greater the dilution of earnings per share.
   5. The greater the discount, the greater the total amount of dividends the company will have to pay, and the lower its coverage ratio.
   6. For most rights offerings, the subscription price discount from the current market price ranges between 10 and 20 percent.
   7. Other factors which influence the success of a rights offering are:
      a. the size of the capital outlay in relation to a stockholder's existing ownership,
      b. the mix of existing stockholders (large vs. small, individual vs. institutional),

141

                c. the current trend and stability of the stock market.
        E. A company can enhance the chances of a successful rights
           offering in three ways:
           1. having an investment banker "stand by" to underwrite the
              unsold portion of the issue ensures the success of the
              offering.
           2. oversubscriptions give stockholders not only the right
              to subscribe for their proportional share of the total
              offering but also the right to oversubscribe for any
              unsold shares.
           3. a "green shoe" provision gives underwriters the option
              to purchase additional stock at the offering price for
              several weeks after the offering.
        F. There are several advantages of a rights issue over a
           public offering:
           1. the company taps investors who are already familiar with
              the operations of the company,
           2. the flotation costs may be lower,
           3. share prices decline when an amendment to the corporate
              charter to eliminate preemptive rights is announced,
           4. the more concentrated the ownership of a company, the
              lower the expense of a rights offering.
        G. There are also several advantages of a public offering over
           a rights issue:
           1. a rights offering will have to be sold at a lower price
              than will an issue offered to the general public,
           2. there will be more dilution with rights offerings than
              with public issues,
           3. information, legal, and institutional imperfections may
              cause shareholder wealth to be enhanced by a public
              offering,
           4. a public offering will result in a wider distribution of
              shares,
           5. total transactions costs (flotation and price
              concession) are higher for an underwritten rights
              offering than for a public offering.

III. Venture capital represents funds (mostly common stock)
     invested in a new enterprise.
     A. Letter stock is stock that is unregistered when sold, is
        not expected to be registered for years, and therefore
        cannot be resold.
     B. Venture capitalists hope to sell their stock for many times
        what they paid for it, but they accept a large probability
        that they will lose everything.
        1. The keys to success are the quality of management and
           the potential market niche for the product or service.
        2. Wealthy individuals, partnerships, and institutions such
           as pension funds, trusts, life insurance companies, and
           universities are sources of venture capital.
     C. If the private firm is successful, usually the owners will
        take the company public with a sale of stock to outsiders.

1. This initial public offering (IPO) establishes a value, and liquidity, for the stock and allows the venture capitalists to realize a cash return on their investment.
2. The disadvantages of going public include conforming to SEC requirements with respect to organization, disclosure, and accounting conventions.
3. Most IPOs are done though an underwriter with a reputation for neither underpricing the stock too much or too little, relative to the price that will prevail in the aftermarket.

IV. When a public company announces a security issue there may be an information effect that causes a stock price reaction.
   A. Empirical studies have found several different informational effects:
      1. Straight debt and preferred stock cause no statistically significant stock price reactions.
      2. Repurchase of common stock was accompanied by positive abnormal stock returns in the 2 days immediately prior to the announcement; sale of common stock was accompanied by negative abnormal returns.
      3. An exchange offering of one security for another, that increased leverage but did not affect cash flow, was accompanied by positive abnormal stock returns in the 2 days prior to the announcement; leverage-reducing exchanges were accompanied by negative abnormal returns.
      4. This evidence is consistent with an asymmetric information effect:
         a. Managers are more likely to issue debt or preferred when they believe the common stock is underpriced.
         b. They are more likely to issue common stock when it is believed to be overpriced.
   B. In a private sale of stock, a company sells stock to a single investor or to a small group of investors, increasing ownership concentration.
      1. When the level of ownership concentration after the sale is less than 5 percent or more than 25 percent, the announcement effect on stock price is positive.
      2. When the level of ownership concentration after the sale is between 5 percent and 25 percent, the announcement effect on stock price is negative.

MULTIPLE CHOICE QUESTIONS

21.1 The underwriter is paid
   a. a flat fee.
   b. a commission on each share sold.
   c. by buying the stock for a price below what it is expected to sell for.
   d. a fixed fee plus a commission based on sales.

21.2 When an investment banking firm does not actually purchase
the stock, the issue is sold on
a. an underwriting basis.
b. a best efforts basis.
c. a shelf registration basis.
d. a rights basis.

21.3 A shelf registration can be used to cover securities which
the firm plans to issue during the next
a. year.
b. two years.
c. three years.
d. decade.

21.4 The major benefits with shelf registrations for large
companies are
a. reduced time to issue and lower cost.
b. reduced time to issue and more flexibility.
c. reduced risk and lower cost.
d. reduced time to issue and reduced risk.

21.5 Even though the actual time period is usually longer, the
minimum period between registration and the time it can
become effective is
a. 10 days.
b. 20 days.
c. 30 days.
d. 40 days.

21.6 The right granted to stockholders which permits them to
maintain their proportional ownership is called the
a. prime right.
b. proportional right.
c. preemptive right.
d. percentage right.

21.7 On the day the stock goes ex-rights, other things equal,
a. the value of the right increases.
b. the value of the right decreases.
c. the market value of the stock increases.
d. the market value of the stock decreases.

21.8 Theoretically, other things equal, a new stock offering is
more likely to be successful if the
a. subscription price is low.
b. subscription price is high.
c. demand for the stock is low.
d. volatility of the stock price is high.

21.9 The major disadvantage in using a stand-by underwriting arrangement along with a rights issue is
    a. increased risk.
    b. increased cost.
    c. the reduction in rights exercised.
    d. the increase in rights exercised.

21.10 Venture capitalists look for
    a. convertible bonds.
    b. letter stock that is about to be registered.
    c. good management and a strong potential market.
    d. a large proportion of successful investments.

21.11 Initial public offerings do all of the following except
    a. sell stock at or above its true value.
    b. establish liquidity for the stock.
    c. rely on the reputation of the underwriter.
    d. sell at a discount from the after-market price.

21.12 A private sale of stock
    a. is illegal.
    b. tends to increase ownership concentration.
    c. tends to diffuse ownership concentration.
    d. increases stock price because of asymmetric information.

ANSWERS

21.1	c	p.	544
21.2	b	p.	547
21.3	b	p.	548
21.4	a	pp.	547-548
21.5	b	p.	549
21.6	c	p.	550

21.7	d	p.	551
21.8	a	p.	552
21.9	b	p.	555
21.10	c	p.	557
21.11	a	p.	558
21.12	b	p.	561

CHAPTER 22

FIXED-INCOME FINANCING AND PENSION LIABILITY

PERSPECTIVE

When financing with long-term debt, a company must bargain with investors over the terms of the debt instrument. If the company wishes to include terms that are not beneficial to investors, it must pay a higher yield in order to sell the instrument.

The principal features of debt include the return, the maturity, the claim on assets, the credit quality, the call feature, and the presence or absence of a sinking fund. When there is a call feature, one method for analyzing the refunding of the issue before maturity is to treat the refunding operation as a riskless capital budgeting project. An alternative method replicates the cash payment stream on the old bonds and calculates the net cash provided by the refunding.

Rather than offer securities to the general public, a company may place them privately with an institutional investor. There is no underwriting and no SEC registration of the issue.

Preferred stock has characteristics of both debt and common stock. The payment of dividends is the feature that attracts the most attention, although preferred stock can be callable and/or convertible.

Most corporate pension plans involve defined benefits, and the present value of the pension liability must be compared with the present value of assets. If the former exceeds the latter, the company has an unfunded liability which is of great concern to the suppliers of capital.

CHAPTER OUTLINE

I. Long-term debt can have a great variety of features.
   A. The standardized features are:
      1. The debtholders cannot exercise control over the company and do not have a voice in management.
      2. They do not participate in the residual earnings of the company; their return is fixed.
      3. Their security has a specific maturity.
      4. In liquidation, their claim is before that of preferred and common stockholders.
      5. A coupon rate of 9 percent indicates that the issuer will pay bondholders $45 semiannually for every $1,000 face value bond they hold.

6. The yield to maturity is determined by solving for the rate of discount that equates the present value of principal and interest payments with the current market price of the security.
7. A trustee is a financial intermediary designated by the issuing company to represent the interests of the bondholders.
8. The legal agreement between the issuing company and the bondholders is defined in the indenture.
9. Long-term debt may have restrictive covenants, very similar to those contained in a term loan agreement.
10 Publicly traded debt instruments can be rated by Moody's Investors Service and Standard & Poor's.
   a. Bonds rated Ba/BB or less are called "junk" or "high-yield" bonds.
   b. They were used in acquisitions and leveraged buyouts.
   c. The active market for these bonds that developed in the 1980s has all but disappeared as the default rate increased at the end of the decade.
B. Optional features include the following:
1. A sinking fund provision requires the corporation to make periodic payments to the trustee, in order to retire a specified face amount of bonds each period.
   a. The corporation can make a cash payment to the trustee, who retires specific bonds by a lottery method, and pays the bondholder the face value.
   b. If the market price of the bonds is less than the sinking fund call price, the company can buy bonds in the open market and deliver them to the trustee.
2. The interest rate on floating rate notes can vary with some short-term rate such as the Treasury bill or commercial paper rate.
3. A call feature gives the corporation the option to buy back the bonds at a stated price before they mature.
   a. The call price is usually above the par value of the bond and declines over time.
   b. The bonds may be callable immediately or the call provision may be deferred for a period of time.
   c. The call feature gives the company the flexibility to refinance if interest rates fall or the bond contains any unduly restrictive covenants.
   d. The yield on a callable bond is higher than the yield on a noncallable bond.
   e. When interest rates are high and expected to fall, the call feature is valuable; when they are low and expected to rise, it is not.
   f. The greater the variance or uncertainty of future interest rates, the greater the value of the call option to the company, and the higher its cost.

C. There are several types of debt financing.
   1. Debentures are the unsecured bonds of a corporation; they are backed by the earning power of the company.
      a. Senior debentures must be paid in full before the subordinated debentures receive anything when the firm is liquidated.
      b. The yield on subordinated debentures is higher than the yield on senior debentures if both are nonconvertible.
   2. Mortgage bonds are secured by a lien on specific fixed assets of the corporation.
      a. The mortgage is the legal document giving the bondholder a lien on the property, and describing it in detail.
      b. When the firm is liquidated, the proceeds from the mortgaged assets are used to pay off the mortgage bondholders; if the proceeds are insufficient, the bondholders become general creditors for the residual amount.
      c. There may be more than one mortgage on a specific asset, but the first mortgage holders must be paid in full before the second mortgage holders receive anything.
   3. Income bonds arise from corporate reorganizations.
      a. A company is obliged to pay interest on an income bond only when it is earned.
      b. There may or may not be a cumulative feature with respect to unpaid interest.
   4. Equipment trust certificates are used by railroads to finance the acquisition of rolling stock.
      a. Title to the new equipment is held by a trustee who leases it to the railroad, usually for 15 years.
      b. The railroad's lease payments are used by the trustee to pay a fixed return on the outstanding certificates and to retire a specified portion of them at regular intervals.
      c. Airlines use a form of equipment trust certificate to finance jet aircraft.
   5. Convertible bonds may be changed, at the option of the holder, into a specified number of shares of common stock of the issuing corporation.
   6. Project financing includes a variety of financing arrangements for large, individual investment projects.
      a. A separate legal entity may be formed to own the project; suppliers of capital look to the project's earnings for repayment of their loan or for the return on their equity.
      b. A consortium of companies may be formed to spread risk and to share equity participation in the project; the rest of the capital comes from lenders or lessors.

c. If the loan/lease is on a nonrecourse basis, the risk to the lender/lessor depends on the economic feasibility of the project and the size of the equity participation.

d. Alternatively, each sponsor may guarantee its share of the project's obligations; the lender/lessor then depends on the economic feasibility of the project and the creditworthiness of the sponsors.

II. Refunding means calling a bond issue and replacing it with a new bond issue to take advantage of a decline in interest rates or to eliminate an overly restrictive protective covenant.

A. The bond should be called if the present value of future interest savings is greater than the initial cash outlay of calling the bonds.

1. The initial cash outflow equals:
   a. the difference between the call price of the old bond issue and the net proceeds of the new bond issue,
   b. plus the issuing expense of the new bonds,
   c. plus the interest expense on the old bonds during the days/weeks when both are outstanding,
   d. less the tax savings on the interest expense on the old bonds during the overlap period,
   e. less the tax savings on the call premium,
   f. less the tax savings on the unamortized discount and issuing expense on the old bonds,
   g. plus the after-tax interest earned on the investment of the proceeds of the new bond issue during the overlap period.

2. The annual net cash benefits equal the difference between the net cash outflows required on the old and new bonds; these outflows are:
   a. the annual interest expense,
   b. less the tax savings on the interest expense,
   c. less the tax savings on the amortization of the bond discount,
   d. less the tax savings on the amortization of the issuing costs.

3. Since the refunding operation is essentially a riskless investment project, the appropriate discount rate is the cost of debt.
   a. There is disagreement as to whether the before-tax or after-tax cost should be used.
   b. The text does not choose between them.

4. The procedure needs to be modified if:
   a. the new bond does not mature when the old one would have.
   b. neither issue involved sinking-fund bonds or serial bonds.
   c. leverage is not held constant.

B. An alternative way to evaluate the refunding decision is to replicate the cash outflows of the old bond issue and then determine the net inflow to be realized from the sale of the new bonds in the current market.
   1. If the new bonds can be sold so that the net inflow exceeds the outflow associated with calling the old bonds, the refunding should be done; if the net inflow is less, the refunding should not be done.
   2. The stream of future net cash outflows from the old bond, discounted at the yield to maturity of the new bond, less the underwriting spread, equals the net proceeds of the new bond issue.
   3. The net cash inflow from the sale of the new bonds is:
      a. the net proceeds of the new bond issue,
      b. less the cost of calling the old bonds,
      c. less the interest expense on the old bonds during the overlap period,
      d. plus the tax savings on the interest expense on the old bonds during the overlap period,
      e. plus the tax savings on the call premium.
C. Both refunding methods assume that the refunding will be undertaken right away.
   1. If interest rates are declining, and this decline is expected to continue, the refunding should be delayed.
   2. In deciding whether or not to postpone refunding, the financial manager should consider the dispersion and shape of the probability distribution of future interest rates.

III. In a private placement, a company sells the entire issue to a single institutional investor or to a small group of such investors, negotiating the terms directly and eliminating the function of the underwriter.
A. A private placement issue avoids the delay of registration with the SEC, which now permits institutional investors to sell privately-placed securities to other large institutions.
B. It also avoids the public disclosure of information required by the SEC.
C. While it is easier to change any of the terms of a private placement if such a change becomes necessary, the lender may monitor the company's operations more carefully than would the trustee for a public issue.
D. The money need not be borrowed all at once, but the borrower usually will pay a commitment fee for this nonrevolving credit arrangement.
E. If the company has to be restructured, public bonds become less creditworthy and drop in price, but privately placed bonds contain protective covenants that make the bonds immediately payable at their face value.
F. Public issues of bonds tend to bear a lower interest rate than private placements.

IV. Preferred stock is a hybrid form of financing, combining features of debt and common stock.
   A. In case of liquidation, preferred stockholders' claim on assets comes after creditors' but before that of common stockholders.
   B. The unique feature of preferred stock is its dividend.
      1. The maximum dividend is fixed, but the actual payment is at the discretion of the board of directors.
      2. Almost all preferred stocks are cumulative, meaning that before the company can pay a dividend on its common stock, it must pay all dividends in arrears on its preferred stock.
      3. If the company has no intention of paying a common stock dividend, there is no need to clear up the arrearage on the preferred.
      4. If a preferred stock is noncumulative, dividends not paid in one year do not carry forward.
      5. A participating feature allows preferred stockholders to participate in any extraordinary earnings of the company, according to some specified formula.
      6. Preferred stockholders normally do not have a voice in management unless the company is unable to pay preferred dividends for a specified number of quarters; then they are entitled to elect a relatively small number of directors (usually two).
      7. Dividends are not a tax-deductible expense.
   C. Provision is usually made for the retirement of preferred stock.
      1. Because the market price of preferred stock tends to fluctuate counter to interest rate cycles, most preferred stock issues have a call feature like bonds.
      2. A company can retire noncallable preferred only by the relatively expensive methods of:
         a. purchasing the stock in the open market,
         b. inviting tenders from the stockholders at a price above the market price, or
         c. offering the preferred stockholders another security in exchange.
      3. Many preferred stock issues provide for a sinking fund, which partially assures an orderly retirement of the stock.
      4. Convertible preferred stock is used frequently in the acquisition of other companies.
         a. It is used because the transaction is not taxable for the company that is acquired, or for its stockholders, at the time of acquisition; it becomes a taxable transaction only when the preferred stock is sold.
         b. Because virtually all convertible securities have a call feature, the company can force conversion by calling the preferred stock if its market price is significantly above its call price.

5. For a corporate investor, preferred stock may be more attractive than debt instruments because 70 percent of the dividends received is not subject to taxation.
D. Money market preferred stock has a floating dividend rate; its rate is set by auction every 49 days.
E. From the standpoint of creditors, preferred stock adds to the equity base of the company and thereby strengthens its financial condition; it enhances the company's ability to borrow in the future.

V. Although it does not appear on the balance sheet, many companies have a contractual obligation to make present and future pension payments.
A. Under the Employee Retirement Income Security Act of 1975 (ERISA), this liability is senior to all other claims in liquidation.
B. Corporate pension plans may be one of two types.
1. A defined benefit plan either pays a retired employee so many dollars per month (a flat benefit formula) or it pays the retiree a percentage of his average final salaries (a unit benefit formula).
2. In a defined contribution plan, a company makes a specified monthly or annual tax-deductible payment to the pension plan, these payments (plus voluntary contributions by the employee) are invested, and at retirement the employee is entitled to the cumulative total of contributions plus investment earnings.
C. An unfunded pension liability must be reported on the balance sheet as a liability.
1. The unfunded pension liability equals the present value of pension liabilities less the present value of pension assets; if this difference is negative, nothing appears on the balance sheet.
2. The present value of liabilities is the discounted value of likely future benefits to be paid, where these benefits are based on:
a. the average life expectancy of currently retired employees,
b. the benefits earned by current employees by virtue of past employment, and
c. the likely benefits to be earned by current employees based on a forecast of future service.
3. The magnitude of the present value is sensitive to the discount rate employed; the higher the rate, the lower the liability.
a. The rate must correspond to a realistic return on investment in stocks, bonds, and other assets.
b. Actuaries are usually conservative in the rate they use.
c. Auditors and government agencies restrict the degree to which "creative" actuarial changes can occur.

4. The present value of the assets consists of two parts:
    a. past corporate contributions paid to a trust or insurance company and invested in a diversified portfolio of assets at market value,
    b. the present value of expected future contributions by the company for future service by employees.
5. If an underfunded pension plan is terminated, the company is responsible for the deficit up to 30 percent of its net worth.

D. If a company should go into bankruptcy and there are insufficient funds on hand to meet its pension obligations, the Pension Benefit Guarantee Corporation makes good on most of the total obligation.
1. This government agency is funded by premiums paid by companies with pension plans.
2. The premium is invariant with respect to default risk.

E. When interest rates decline and actuarial assumptions result in a plan being overfunded, many companies voluntarily terminate their plans and start new ones. The "excess overfunding" in the old plan then reverts to the company, boosting earnings and net worth.

F. Unions have their own pension plans and the labor contracts they negotiate with corporations include contributions to the union pension fund.

G. The cash actually contributed to a pension plan for the year is usually different from the pension expense recorded according to FASB 87:
1. the interest cost, which is the interest rate times the pension liability,
2. plus the service cost for additional benefits employees earn during the year,
3. plus amortization of any unfunded liability,
4. less the expected investment return.

H. The financial manager is responsible for:
1. determining asset allocations,
2. choosing investment managers,
3. monitoring investment performance,
4. analyzing actuarial assumptions,
5. determining the proper funding of a plan,
6. overseeing the record keeping of the fund.

APPENDIX:
It is possible to hedge fixed-income instruments by using interest-rate futures, debt options, and interest-rate swaps.
A. A financial futures contract is a standardized agreement that calls for delivery of a security at some specified future date.
1. Futures contracts are available for Eurodollars, Treasury bills, notes and bonds, and municipal bonds.
2. Hedging represents taking a future contract position opposite to a position taken in the spot market.

153

3. A long hedge involves buying a futures contract because the investor believes interest rates have peaked at present and wishes to lock in the current high rates even though funds will not be available for investment for a short period into the future.
4. A short hedge involves selling a futures contract now instead of selling an actual security held, because the investor believes that interest rates are about to rise.
5. A cross hedge involves using a Treasury bond futures contract to hedge an investment in long-term corporate bonds because there is no corporate bond futures contract.

B. There are exchange markets for options on futures contracts for Eurodollars, Treasury bills, notes and bonds, and on the municipal bond futures index.
1. When buying an option, the hedger's potential loss is limited to the premium paid; there is no such limit when hedging with a futures contract.
2. Options are particularly suited to hedging risk in one direction; one can buy or write either calls or puts.

C. An interest rate swap is an exchange of interest payment obligations, usually between a floating rate and a fixed rate.
1. A corporation that has borrowed on a fixed-rate, term basis may swap with a corporation that has borrowed directly on a floating-rate basis.
2. The company that owes more interest than it receives in the swap pays the difference.
3. There is no transfer of principal; only the interest obligation is exchanged.
4. Often an intermediary, a commercial or investment bank, makes the arrangements and the counterparties to the swap do not know each other.
5. Intermediaries have assumed the default risk.
6. Most default risk is on the fixed rate side, and then only if interest rates decline.
7. The interest rate futures and debt options markets extend out only 2 or 3 years; the swap market provides hedges for longer maturities.

MULTIPLE CHOICE QUESTIONS

22.1 The interest rate stated on the bond is also referred to as
a. the coupon rate.
b. the internal rate of return.
c. the yield.
d. the discount rate.

22.2 The legal agreement between the firm and the trustee representing the bondholders is called the bond
a. covenant.
b. agreement.
c. indenture.
d. contract.

22.3 Low grade or non-investment grade bonds (rated Ba or lower) are referred to as
a. trash bonds.
b. junk bonds.
c. default bonds.
d. creditless bonds.

22.4 A bond that has no property pledged as collateral is
a. a debenture.
b. an indenture.
c. a serial bond.
d. a sinking fund bond.

22.5 The corporate bond feature which permits the firm to buy back bonds prior to their maturity is referred to as the
a. refunding privilege.
b. call privilege.
c. refinancing privilege.
d. retirement privilege.

22.6 Which of the following cannot be expensed immediately on a bond refunding?
a. discount on new bonds
b. unamortized discount on old bonds
c. call premium
d. interest on old bonds during overlap period

22.7 The major advantage of a private placement is
a. reduced cost.
b. reduced risk.
c. investor monitoring potential.
d. flexibility.

22.8 The dominant type of lender in the private placement market is
a. commercial banks.
b. mutual funds.
c. insurance companies.
d. pension funds.

22.9 From the issuing firm's standpoint, the major disadvantage of preferred stock is
      a. risk.
      b. cost.
      c. flexibility.
      d. maturity.

22.10 The present value of pension liabilities is the discounted value of likely future benefits to be paid, where these benefits are based on all of the following except
      a. the average life expectancy of currently retired employees.
      b. the benefits earned by current union employees by virtue of past employment.
      c. the benefits earned by current employees by virtue of past employment.
      d. the likely benefits to be earned by current employees based on a forecast of future service.

ANSWERS

22.1	a	p.	566		22.6	a	p.	577
22.2	c	p.	567		22.7	d	pp.	581-582
22.3	b	p.	568		22.8	c	p.	581
22.4	a	p.	570		22.9	b	p.	585
22.5	b	p.	573		22.10	b	p.	587

CHAPTER 23

OPTION FINANCING:
WARRANTS, CONVERTIBLES, AND EXCHANGEABLES

PERSPECTIVE

Warrants, convertible securities, and exchangeable securities are options under which the holder can obtain common stock.

Warrants are the most similar to call options, but they have a longer time to expiration and their exercise dilutes earnings per share. They are issued as an inducement to purchase the security to which they are attached.

Convertible bonds or preferred stock are a way of delaying common stock financing and reducing the amount of dilution. The premium at which a convertible security sells above its conversion value and bond value is caused by the security's partial downside protection as a bond and its upside potential as a stock.

An exchangeable bond may be exchanged for common stock in another corporation in which the issuing company owns shares. It is a way of reducing the interest cost and disposing of the other company's shares at a premium.

CHAPTER OUTLINE

I. A warrant is an option to purchase a specified number of shares of common stock at a stated price until a stated expiration date, (perpetual warrants have no expiration date).
   A. Because warrants increase in value as the price of the underlying common stock rises, they usually originate from one of two different events.
      1. They are often employed as "sweeteners" to a public issue of bonds or to debt that is privately placed.
      2. They are used in the founding of a company as compensation to underwriters and venture capitalists.
   B. Because a warrant is only an option to purchase stock, warrant holders are not entitled to any cash dividends paid on the common stock, nor do they have voting power.
   C. If the common stock is split or a stock dividend is declared, the option price of the warrant usually is adjusted to take this change into account.
   D. A company with warrants outstanding is required to report both primary earnings per share and fully diluted earnings per share.
   E. When warrants are exercised, three things happen:
      1. The common stock of the company is increased.

2. The debt that was issued in conjunction with the warrants remains outstanding, assuming the warrants are detachable.
3. The company gets an infusion of new capital (the exercise price times the number of shares purchased).
F. A company cannot force the exercise of a warrant.
G. The theoretical value of a warrant is calculated as $NP_s - E$, where,
   - N = number of shares purchased with one warrant,
   - P_s = market price of one share of stock,
   - E = exercise dollar amount associated with the purchase of N shares.
H. If the Black-Scholes option pricing formula is used to value a warrant, certain adjustments are necessary if the number of new shares issued is relatively large.

II. A convertible security is a bond or a share of preferred stock that can be converted at the option of the holder into common stock of the same corporation.
A. The conversion privilege can be stated in terms of either the conversion price or the conversion ratio:
   $FV/CP = CR$, or $FV/CR = CP$, where,
   - FV = face value of the convertible security,
   - CR = Conversion Ratio (the number of shares of common stock into which the security can be exchanged),
   - CP = Conversion Price (the stated price of the common stock at conversion).
B. The conversion price is adjusted for stock splits or stock dividends (the antidilution clause) and may be stepped up at periodic intervals to stimulate (but not force) conversion. Both provisions must be established at the time the issue is sold.
C. The conversion value of a convertible security is the conversion ratio of the security times the market price per share of the common stock.
   1. At the time of issuance, the convertible security will be priced higher than its conversion value, and the difference is known as the conversion premium.
   2. Because of the potential for capital gains, the yield on a convertible security is lower than it would have been on a straight security.
   3. Most convertible securities are callable, allowing the company to force conversion when the conversion value of the security is above its call price.
   4. Forcing conversion may be necessary because investors may prefer to hold the convertible security.
      a. The price of the convertible will increase as the price of the common increases.
      b. The interest or preferred dividend may be greater than or equal to the common dividend.

      c. The commission on the ultimate sale of the convertible security will be less than the commission on the common stock.
D. Almost all convertible bond issues are subordinated to other creditors.
E. As with warrants, it is necessary for companies to report both primary and fully diluted earnings per share.
    1. By selling a convertible security instead of common stock, the company creates less dilution of earnings per share both now and in the future.
    2. Dilution is minimized because the conversion price on a convertible security is higher than the issuing price of a new issue of common stock.
F. A convertible bond may be viewed as straight debt plus a warrant to purchase common stock if the following conditions hold:
    1. The conversion ratio and the relative number of warrants are the same.
    2. The warrants are not detachable from the debt.
    3. The straight debt's maturity, the expiration date of the warrant, and the maturity of the convertible are all the same.
    4. The coupon rates and redemption features are the same.
G. The bond value of a convertible security is the price at which a straight bond of the same company would sell in the open market, and can be determined by solving the following equation for B:

$$B = \sum_{t=1}^{2n} I/(1 + i/2)^t + F/(1 + i/2)^{2n}, \text{ where,}$$

    B = straight bond value of the convertible,
    I = semiannual interest payments (1/2 the coupon rate),
    F = face value of the bond,
    n = years to final maturity,
    i = market yield to maturity on a straight bond issued by the same company.
H. The bond value floor of a convertible is not constant over time.
    1. If interest rates in general rise, the bond value will decline, and vice versa.
    2. As the company's credit rating improves, its financial risk declines, and its bond value will increase. If its credit rating deteriorates, its financial risk increases, and its bond value will decline.
I. Convertible securities frequently sell at a premium over both their bond value and their conversion value for several reasons.
    1. They offer the holder partial protection on the downside together with participation in upward movements in stock price.

2. Certain institutional investors are restricted with respect to investing in common stock and convertible bonds give them the benefits of a common stock investment.
3. The smaller the dividend on the common stock, the less attractive the common relative to the convertible, and the higher the premiums.

III. An exchangeable bond is like a convertible bond, but the common stock involved is that of another corporation.
   A. The exchange price, exchange ratio, and exchange premium are set at the time of issuance.
   B. There typically is a call feature with an exchangeable bond, and most issues are subordinated.
   C. Exchangeable bond issues usually occur only when the issuer owns common stock in the company for which the bonds can be exchanged, and this decision may result in the reduction or elimination of stock ownership in that company at a premium above the present price.
   D. Interest costs are lower because of the option value of the exchangeable bond.
   E. The value of exchangeable debt equals the value of the debt plus the call option on the stock of the company for which the debt is exchangeable.
   F. One advantage of the exchangeable bond is diversification; poor earnings and financial performance in one company will not lead to a simultaneous decline in both the bond-value floor and the stock value because the two are not directly linked.
   G. One disadvantage is that the difference between the market value of the stock at the time of exchange and the cost of the bond when purchased is treated as a capital gain for tax purposes.

APPENDIX
   The greater the volatility of the stock and the underlying volatility of firm value, the greater the value of the conversion option to the convertible security holder.
   A. If the financial markets were perfect, and if a firm had no debt other than convertible bonds, optimal strategies for the bondholders and the firm would be:
      1. Bondholders would convert their bonds into stock if the value of the convertible were less than its conversion value.
      2. Bondholders would force the firm into bankruptcy and seize its value if the value of the firm fell below the debt's face value.
      3. The firm would call the bonds when their value equalled the call price.
   B. Given the above scenario, the lower boundaries for the value of convertible bonds would be the face value of the bonds until exceeded by the conversion value; the upper

boundaries would be the call price as long as it exceeded the value of the firm and was less than the conversion value.
C. Within these boundaries, the exact value of the bonds would depend on:
a. the inverse relationship between the risk of default and the value of the firm,
b. the expected level and volatility of interest rates,
c. the volatility of the common stock into which the bond can be converted, and
d. the interrelationships among these variables.

MULTIPLE CHOICE QUESTIONS

23.1 Which of the following decreases the value of a warrant?
a. an increase in the variance of the stock price
b. an increase in the price of the stock
c. increased dividends
d. increased duration of option period

23.2 Most warrants are
a. sweeteners.
b. callable.
c. perpetual.
d. non-dilutive.

23.3 Attaching warrants to bonds should
a. increase the risk of the bonds.
b. decrease the risk of the bonds.
c. increase the interest rate on the bonds.
d. decrease the interest rate on the bonds.

23.4 The exercise of a warrant results in
a. an increase in the assets of the firm.
b. an increase in the value per share.
c. a decrease in the number of shares of common.
d. no change in the number of shares of common.

23.5 A $1,000 bond is convertible into 40 shares of common stock. The current market price of the stock is $30 per share. The conversion value is
a. $25.
b. $750.
c. $1,000.
d. $1,200.

23.6 Most convertible securities
a. are not subordinated.
b. are not callable.
c. are not perpetual.
d. have higher interest rates than straight debt.

23.7 Most bonds which are forced into conversion are forced by means of
   a. paying higher dividends on the stock.
   b. stepping-up the conversion price.
   c. splitting the stock.
   d. calling the bonds.

23.8 The bond-value floor of a convertible bond
   a. is $1,000.
   b. changes with interest rate movements.
   c. is the number of shares times the price per share.
   d. is constant.

23.9 As the market price of the stock increases, the premium over conversion value
   a. decreases.
   b. stays the same.
   c. increases.
   d. fluctuates randomly.

23.10 Exchangeable bonds can be exchanged for
   a. bonds of another firm.
   b. preferred stock of the issuing firm.
   c. common stock of the issuing firm.
   d. common stock of another firm.

ANSWERS

23.1 c p.   604
23.2 a p.   604
23.3 d p.   605
23.4 a p.   605
23.5 b pp. 608-609   ($1,000)($30)/$40 = $750

23.6 c pp. 608-609
23.7 d p.   611
23.8 b p.   614
23.9 a p.   615
23.10 d p.   617

CHAPTER 24

MERGERS AND THE MARKET FOR CORPORATE CONTROL

PERSPECTIVE

One company may acquire another through the purchase of its assets or its stock, and payment can be cash or stock. Alternatively, two companies may combine to produce a new entity. Tax and accounting considerations are important.

When evaluating a potential acquisition, the effect on earnings per share, revenues, costs, taxes, management, cash flow stability, and share price must be considered.

Corporate voting determines whether a merger attempt will be successful. Common stockholders elect the board of directors by proxy, using either a majority or a cumulative voting system. Proxy contests are one means by which outsiders can seize corporate control.

A company can defend itself against a takeover attempt in several ways both before and while it is happening. Empirical studies have examined the results of successful and failed takeover attempts and the effectiveness of antitakeover devices.

CHAPTER OUTLINE

I. Corporate takeovers can be both good and bad.
   A. Competition among management teams to control corporate resources may motivate better management throughout the economy.
   B. In an era of great merger activity, management is consumed with short-term strategies involving potential takeovers and possible defenses against being taken over, to the detriment of the long-run viability of the enterprise.
   C. The value of a combined company is the sum of the values of the parts plus any synergy (economies realized in the merger through increased revenues and/or cost reductions) that might be involved:
   $V_{AB} = V_A + V_B +$ Synergy, where
      V_{AB} = value of company after the merger,
      V_A = value of company A before the merger,
      V_B = value of company B before the merger,
   D. During a takeover frenzy, irrational prices may be paid for corporate control; company A may be willing to pay more than $V_{AB} - V_A$ for company B.

II. There are many important distinctions among merger activities.
   A. There are two distinctions based upon the outcome of the combination of companies.
      1. A merger is a combination of two corporations in which only one survives.
      2. A consolidation is a combination of two corporations in which neither survives, but an entirely new company is formed.
      3. A takeover can mean a friendly merger or an unfriendly acquisition.
   B. There are three distinctions based upon the types of companies being combined.
      1. A horizontal merger combines two companies in the same line of business.
      2. In a vertical merger, a company either expands forward toward the ultimate consumer or backward toward the source of raw material.
      3. A conglomerate merger combines two companies in unrelated lines of business.
   C. A company may use cash or its own securities to purchase:
      1. the common stock of another company, in which case the acquired company ceases to exist;
      2. all the assets but not the liabilities of another company, in which case the selling company may:
         a. hold the cash or securities and continue to exist,
         b. sell the securities and/or invest the cash in other assets and continue to exist,
         c. distribute the cash or securities to its stockholders as a liquidating dividend, after which it ceases to exist.
      3. only a portion of the assets of another company, in which case the seller will continue as a corporate entity.
   D. How the purchase is made has both tax and stock price implications.
      1. If the acquisition is made with cash or with a debt instrument, the transaction is taxable to the selling company or its stockholders at that time.
      2. If payment is made with voting preferred or common stock, the transaction is not taxable at the time of the sale if certain IRS standards are met.
      3. Empirical evidence suggests that acquiring company stockholders realize lower returns upon the announcement of an equity-financed merger than they do when a cash merger is announced.
   E. Accountants may treat a combination of two companies as either:
      1. a purchase, in which the acquired company is an investment for the buyer.
         a. Tangible assets must be reported at fair market value.

b. The difference between the price paid and the value of the assets must be shown as goodwill on the balance sheet and written off against future income.
  2. a pooling of interests, where the balance sheets of the two companies are combined by simple addition and there is no goodwill.
     a. A merger may be treated as a pooling of interests only under a set of restrictive conditions.
     b. One of these conditions is the rule that the acquiring corporation can issue only common stock, in exchange for at least 90 percent of the outstanding common stock of the acquiree.
  F. The motivation behind an acquisition is important.
     1. A strategic acquisition occurs when one company acquires another as part of its overall strategy, and it will blend the two to obtain cost advantages or revenue enhancement.
     2. A financial acquisition occurs when a financial promoter acquires a company to sell off its assets, cut costs, and operate whatever remains more efficiently than before.
        a. The deal invariably involves cash.
        b. The cash is raised largely by debt, which makes it a leveraged buy out (LBO).

III. In evaluating a strategic acquisition, the acquiring firm must consider the effect on earnings per share (EPS).
  A. The merger may have any one of a number of different effects on the (EPS) of the surviving corporation.
     1. Dilution of the acquiring company's EPS will occur any time the price-earnings ratio (P/E) paid for a company exceeds the P/E of the acquiring company.
     2. The higher the P/E of the acquiring company above the P/E of the acquired company, and the larger the earnings of the acquired company relative to those of the acquiring company, the greater the increase in EPS for the acquiring company.
     3. If the growth in earnings of the surviving company exceeds the growth in earnings the acquiring company expected without the merger, initial dilution of EPS may be acceptable.
     4. Some companies set a ceiling on the number of years dilution will be tolerated, no matter how high the growth rate that follows.
  B. The major emphasis in the bargaining process is on the ratio of exchange of market prices per share.
     1. The ratio of exchange is simply $(P_A)(N)/P_B$, where,
        P_A = market price per share of acquiring company,
        N = number of shares offered,
        P_B = market price per share of acquired company.

2. The acquiring company must offer a ratio greater than 1.00 to entice the shareholders to accept the offer.
3. Companies with high P/Es can acquire companies with lower P/Es and obtain an immediate increase in share price, despite paying an exchange ratio greater than 1.00, if the P/E stays the same after the merger.
   a. This is known as bootstrapping EPS, and works in the absence of synergy, improved management, and the underpricing of the acquired company's stock in an inefficient market.
   b. An acquiring company can show a steady growth in EPS if, over time, it acquires a sufficient number of companies in this manner.
4. If the market is relatively free from imperfections, and if synergy and improved management are not anticipated, the P/E of the surviving firm should approach a weighted average of the two previous P/Es.
   a. The acquisition of companies with lower P/Es would not enhance shareholder wealth.
   b. If the exchange ratio were greater than 1.00, there would be a transfer of wealth from the stockholders of the acquiring company to those of the acquired firm.
C. Other factors may create or rearrange value in the merged firm.
   1. An important reason for some acquisitions is the cost-effective enhancement of sales.
      a. Market dominance may be achieved by gaining market share.
      b. The acquisition may bring technological advances.
      c. The acquisition may fill a gap in the product line, enhancing sales throughout.
   2. Operating economies can often be achieved through a combination of companies.
      a. Duplicate facilities can be eliminated.
      b. Marketing, accounting, purchasing, and other operations can be consolidated.
      c. The sales force may be reduced to avoid duplication of effort in a particular territory.
      d. Economies of scale (average cost declines with increases in volume) may be possible with a merger of two companies in the same line of business.
   3. To the extent that the acquirer can provide better management, an acquisition may make sense for this reason alone.
   4. A merger/takeover attempt provides information on the underlying profitability of the acquiree, giving the market a positive signal and creating value.
   5. The market value of some companies is considerably below the replacement value of their assets, so another company wishing to invest in those assets finds it cheaper to acquire than to build from scratch.

6. A company with cumulative tax losses may have little prospect of earning enough in the future to fully utilize its tax-loss carryforward without merging with a profitable company.
7. By acquiring a firm in a different line of business, a company may be able to reduce cyclical instability in earnings.
   a. To the extent that the combination lowers the relative variability of cash flows, debt holders benefit in having a more creditworthy claim.
   b. The market value of the debt should increase, and wealth may be transferred from equity holders to debt holders if the value of the firm does not increase.

D. It is possible that a merger may reduce the value of the acquiring firm's stock.
   1. The hubris hypothesis suggests that an excessive premium paid for the target company benefits those stockholders, but the stockholders of the acquiring company suffer a diminution in wealth.
      a. "Hubris" refers to an animal-like spirit of arrogant pride and self-confidence.
      b. Bidders with hubris may get caught up in the "heat of the hunt" and pay too much for their targets.
   2. The acquiring company may overpay because management pursues personal as opposed to corporate goals.
      a. Sometimes management chases growth, for the prestige that comes with being large.
      b. Management may wish to diversify because with risk spread out over unrelated businesses, executive jobs may be more secure.
      c. Management whose performance has been poor may seek the bootstrap effect of a merger on EPS.
      d. From the point of view of the acquiree, the owners of a tightly held company may want to be acquired by another company that has an established market for its stock, either to improve their liquidity or to hold shares of stock whose market value is established for estate tax purposes.

IV. Because common stockholders are the owners of the company, they are entitled to elect a board of directors which, in turn, selects the management.
   A. In a proprietorship, partnership, or small corporation, the owners usually directly control the operations of the business; in a large corporation, management may be able to exercise effective control of operations with only a moderate percentage of the stock outstanding.
   B. Control is valuable because management can enjoy private benefits such as high salaries, extensive perquisites, and entrenchment, which work to the disadvantage of public stockholders.

167

C. The corporate charter specifies the voting system to be used to elect the board of directors.
   1. Under a majority system, stockholders have one vote for each share of stock they own.
      a. They must vote for each director position that is open.
      b. Each person seeking a position on the board must win a majority of the total votes cast for that position.
      c. The system precludes minority interests from electing directors.
      d. If management can obtain proxies for over 50 percent of the shares voted, it can select the entire board.
   2. Under a cumulative voting system, a stockholder's total number of votes is the number of shares owned times the number of directors being elected.
      a. The votes can be cast for less than the total number of directors being elected.
      b. The system permits minority interests to elect a certain number of directors.
      c. The minimum number of shares necessary to elect a specific number of directors is determined by:
         $[(S)(N)/(D + 1)] + 1$, where,
            S = total shares outstanding,
            N = specific number of directors sought,
            D = total number of directors to be elected.
      d. Some states require that companies incorporated in that state use a cumulative voting system because it is more democratic.
      e. Management can sometimes preclude minority interests from obtaining a seat on the board of directors by either reducing the size of the board or staggering the terms of the directors so that only a few are elected each year.
D. Voting may be either in person at the stockholders' annual meeting or by proxy.
   1. A proxy is a form that a stockholder signs, giving his right to vote to another person(s).
   2. The SEC regulates the solicitation of proxies and also requires companies to disseminate information to its stockholders through proxy mailings.
   3. If stockholders are satisfied with the company, they generally sign the proxy, giving written authorization to management to vote their shares.
   4. Outsiders can seize control of a company through a proxy contest, but the odds favor existing management to win.
      a. When an outsider undertakes a proxy fight, it is required to register its proxy statement with the SEC to prevent the presentation of misleading or false information.

b. Outsiders are likely to be successful only when the earnings performance of the company has been bad and management is obviously ineffective.

c. A proxy contest often is associated with higher share price performance than otherwise would be the case.

E. To retain control for management, founders, or for some other group, a company may have more than one class of common stock.

1. Class A common may have inferior voting privileges but may be entitled to a prior claim to dividends, while the Class B common has superior voting rights but a lower claim to dividends.

2. Usually the Class A common is sold to the public, and the Class B common is sold or given to the founders and/or promoters and/or management of the company.

3. Empirical studies have shown that the superior voting rights stock tends to trade at a premium above the class of common having inferior voting power.

V. A tender offer is an offer to purchase shares of stock of another company at a fixed price per share from stockholders who "tender" their shares.

A. In both cash and stock tenders, a substantial premium is offered over the existing market price of the stock.

1. Tender offers can be used as a threat during, or in place of, negotiations with the management of the company being acquired.

2. The SEC requires extensive disclosure of tender offers before they are made.

3. A two-tier tender offer involves a more attractive offer for the first tier, which represents control, than for the second tier, which represents the remaining stock.

a. The differential is designed to increase the probability of successfully gaining control, by providing an incentive to tender early.

b. It avoids the problem of individual stockholders who hold out in the hope of getting a higher counteroffer from someone else.

B. The company being bid for may use a number of defensive tactics.

1. Management may try to persuade stockholders that the bid is too low in relation to the true, long-run value of the firm.

2. Some companies raise the cash dividend or declare a stock split.

3. Legal actions to delay and frustrate the bidder may be undertaken.

4. When the two firms are competitors, an antitrust suit may be a powerful deterrent to the bidder.

5. As a last resort, management of the potential acquiree may seek a merger with a friendly company, known as a "white knight."
C. In anticipation of an attempted takeover in the future, some companies put formal defensive tactics in place, called antitakeover or "shark-repellent" devices.
1. Changing the state of incorporation to a state with few limitations makes it easier for a company to install antitakeover amendments as well as to defend itself legally.
2. A super-majority merger approval provision requires that a merger be approved by 2/3 or 4/5 of the directors instead of a simple majority.
3. A fair merger price provision requires the bidder to pay noncontrolling stockholders a price at least equal to a "fair price," which is established in advance.
4. A freeze-out provision allows the transaction to proceed, at a "fair price," only after a delay of between two and five years.
5. Some companies instigate a distribution of rights to shareholders, to be triggered only if an outside party acquires, say, 20 percent of the company's stock.
   a. The new security is often convertible preferred stock.
   b. The new security is made unpalatable to the acquirer and is referred to as a poison pill.
   c. The board reserves the ability to redeem the rights at any time for a token amount.
6. A lock-up provision requires supermajority stockholder approval to modify the corporate charter and any previously passed antitakeover provisions.
7. Management contracts with top executives, providing for high compensation if the company is taken over and they are forced out, are known as golden parachutes.
8. Sometimes the target will negotiate a standstill agreement with the potential acquirer, which is a voluntary contract setting a maximum percentage of stock the acquirer may own for a period of several years.
9. Some companies make a premium buy-back offer to the threatening party, known as greenmail. The repurchase of stock is at a premium over market price and in exchange the accumulator agrees not to buy any more stock in the company for a period of years.
D. When confronted with a hostile takeover, a board of directors must be guided by local and federal laws as interpreted by the courts. While the legal environment differs from state to state, general doctrines of behavior for the board are:
1. It must act in the interests of shareholders and exercise good business judgment.
2. It must act in a way that is fair to all parties, in particular to its shareholders.

3. Its response to a takeover threat must be proportional, with respect to value, to the threat itself.

VI. Recent empirical studies on takeovers make some generalizations possible.
   A. For a completed takeover, the target company stockholders realized appreciable increments in wealth relative to the market value of their holdings prior to any takeover activity.
      1. The wealth increment is due to the premium paid by the acquiring company.
      2. Premiums in the 1980s were nearly double what they were in the 1960s.
      3. Typically, stock price movement begins about 1 month before the announcement.
      4. Share price improvement usually is much greater with a tender offer than with a merger.
   B. For an unsuccessful takeover, the results depend on whether a tender offer or merger was involved.
      1. The target company's share price typically remains high after an unsuccessful tender offer announcement, in anticipation of future tender offers.
      2. If no subsequent acquisition attempts occur, the price slips, possibly back to the preoffer level.
      3. If subsequent bids occur, the share price may go even higher.
      4. The target company's share price typically falls quickly to its preoffer level after an unsuccessful merger is announced.
   C. For the acquiring companies, there are studies which show that the stockholders obtain a small improvement in share price, no change at all, and negative returns. The results are inconclusive.
   D. When the bidder's investment is repurchased by the company (greenmail) or is sold to a third party, stockholders of the acquiring company are rewarded with positive abnormal returns.
   E. Nonconvertible debt holders neither gain nor lose in a merger for both acquiring and acquired companies.
   F. Takeovers have been blamed for lower wages or layoffs for employees, lower prices or renegotiated contracts for suppliers, lower tax revenues for the government, and adverse community effects.
   F. Takeovers and other ownership changes have been credited with higher productivity.
   G. Empirical studies of antitakeover devices have mixed results.
      1. The effectiveness of shark repellents depends on the legal environment.
      2. The use of standstill agreements has a negative effect on stockholder returns.

3. Greenmail appears to hurt nonparticipating stockholders around the time of the announcement.
4. If control subsequently changes hands, stockholders in the corporation that yields to greenmail enjoy positive abnormal returns.
5. The use of a poison pill appears to have a modest negative effect on share price around the time of the announcement; companies that adopt poison pill defenses have been found to be less profitable than other firms in the industry.

MULTIPLE CHOICE QUESTIONS

24.1 When two or more companies combine and an entirely new corporation is formed, the activity is called
a. a takeover.
b. a merger.
c. a consolidation.
d. a tender offer.

24.2 An acquiring company may offer the stockholders of the target company any of the following except
a. cash.
b. commercial paper.
c. convertible preferred stock.
d. common stock.

24.3 Goodwill arises when accountants treat a combination of two companies as
a. a purchase.
b. a pooling of interests.
c. a strategic acquisition.
d. a financial acquisition.

24.4 Shareholders of the target company will not accept a stock-for-stock offer if the ratio of exchange is
a. greater than 2.00
b. equal to 2.00.
c. between 2.00 and 1.00.
d. less than or equal to 1.00.

24.5 Which of the following factors does not create value in a merged firm?
a. market dominance
b. elimination of duplicate facilities
c. removing entrenched management
d. cyclical instability of earnings

24.6 If there are 13 million shares outstanding, 12 directors are to be elected, and a minority group wishes to elect 2 directors, how many shares will it need under a cumulative voting system?
a. 500,001
b. 1,000,001
c. 2,000,001
d. 4,000,001

24.7 When there are two classes of common stock, they generally have
a. equal voting power.
b. equal claims on dividends.
c. equal numbers of shares outstanding.
d. different market prices.

24.8 Which of the following is not a defense tactic against a tender offer?
a. lowering the cash dividend
b. raising the cash dividend
c. splitting the stock
d. seeking a white knight

24.9 Which of the following antitakeover amendments to the company charter may result in an increase in the target company's number of shares outstanding?
a. a super-majority provision
b. a fair merger price provision
c. a freeze-out provision
d. a poison pill

24.10 Greenmail
a. is a shark repellent.
b. is illegal.
c. hurts nonparticipating shareholders.
d. is only payable in Delaware.

ANSWERS

24.1 c p.   631
24.2 b p.   634
24.3 a p.   635
24.4 d pp. 639-640
24.5 d pp. 642-645
24.6 c p.   646 $(13,000,000)(2)/(12+1) + 1 = 2,000,001$

24.7 d p.   648
24.8 a pp. 650-652
24.9 d pp. 650-652
24.10 c pp. 651,656

CHAPTER 25

CORPORATE RESTRUCTURING

PERSPECTIVE

Voluntary divestitures occur to obtain increased efficiency, to correct asymmetric information between investors and management, to transfer wealth, and for tax reasons.

Voluntary liquidations, sell-offs, spin-offs, and equity carveouts have various motivations, but all usually increase shareholder wealth.

When a company goes private, shareholders receive sizeable premiums and the small group of investors accept substantial risk in order to get total control and the hope of large economic gain. A leveraged buyout (LBO) is one method of going private, utilizing huge amounts of senior secured debt and junior subordinated (junk) bonds.

A leveraged recapitalization is similar to an LBO in that massive borrowing is done, but the cash raised through debt is paid out in a large dividend to stockholders. Management receives stock instead of cash, increasing its proportional ownership of the company.

CHAPTER OUTLINE

I. Corporate restructuring can be construed as any major change in capital structure, in operations, or in ownership that is outside the ordinary course of business.
   A. There are different ways a corporation can divest itself of all or part of the enterprise.
      1. An involuntary divestiture usually is the result of an antitrust ruling by the government; a voluntary divestiture is a willful decision by management for one or more reasons.
      2. A corporation may divest itself of an operation because it may be more valuable to someone else in generating cash flows and positive net present value; they are therefore willing to pay a higher price for the operation than its present value to the existing owner.
      3. A corporation may divest itself of one of its own operations or an operation that came with a recent acquisition in the name of "strategic realignment," which means that the operation does not fit into its long-term plans.

174

4. The announcement of a divestiture may have signaling implications.
   a. If the divestiture is announced and/or interpreted as a change in investment strategy or in operating efficiency, share price may go up.
   b. If the divestiture is announced and/or interpreted as the sale of the most marketable subsidiary to deal with adversities elsewhere in the company, share price will go down.
5. If a company divests a portion of the enterprise and distributes the proceeds to stockholders, its remaining collateral value is reduced and there is a wealth transfer from debt holders to stockholders.
6. Sometimes tax considerations enter into a decision to divest.
   a. If a company loses money and is unable to use a tax loss carryforward, divestiture in whole or in part may be the only way to realize value from this tax benefit.
   b. If corporate restructuring involves increased leverage, there is a tax shield advantage associated with interest payments.
   c. With a buyout, a possible tax advantage arises in the use of an employee stock ownership plan (ESOP).
B. A sell-off can consist of the entire company or of some business unit, such as a subsidiary, a division, or a product line.
   1. If the situation does not involve financial failure, the decision to sell a firm in its entirety means that the assets have a higher value to various buyers than the present value of the expected cash-flow stream emanating from them.
      a. If the assets were sold as a whole to one buyer, as in a merger, they may realize a lower value.
      b. With complete liquidation, the debt of the company must be paid off at face value, which may exceed its previous market value. Debt holders realize a wealth gain, which ultimately is at the expense of the stockholders.
   2. If only part of the business is sold, payment generally is in the form of cash or securities, and should result in a greater net present value to the selling company than the present value of the stream of expected future cash flows if the operation were to be continued.
C. Empirical studies of voluntary liquidations and sell-offs examine daily security returns before and after the announcement of the event.
   1. Liquidations result in large abnormal returns to stockholders and an instant significant drop in the stock's beta.
   2. Partial sell-offs frequently follow a period of poor performance for the seller's stock, and usually result

in small positive abnormal returns to the stockholders of both the selling company and the buying company.

II. There are various other divestiture techniques.
  A. A spin-off divests a business unit such as a stand-alone subsidiary or division by distributing common stock in the unit to stockholders of the parent company on a pro rata basis.
    1. The spun-off operation is thereafter a completely separate company with its own traded stock.
    2. Taxation to the stockholder occurs only when the stock is sold.
    3. Empirical studies have found positive abnormal returns associated with spin-offs that are larger than those associated with sell-offs.
  B. An equity carveout involves sale of common stock in the business unit to the public.
    1. The parent company continues to have an equity stake in the subsidiary and does not relinquish control.
    2. The value of the subsidiary becomes observable in the marketplace, and its managers may have more incentive to perform well.
    3. When the subsidiary is in leading edge technology but not particularly profitable, the equity carveout may be a more effective vehicle for financing than is financing through the parent.
    4. Empirically, there is a positive information effect associated with the equity carveout announcement.
  C. Going private means transforming a company whose stock is publicly held into one whose stock is owned by a small group of investors.
    1. Incumbent management usually gets a large equity stake, which tremendously enhances their incentives to make tough decisions and improve performance and profitability.
    2. Most transactions involve cash payment at a premium price to the stockholders, but sometimes noncash compensation, such as notes, is employed.
    3. A majority of the stockholders must agree to a company going private, but a dissident minority can sue for a higher price.
    4. A privately held company avoids both the expenses and the disclosure requirements associated with being publicly held.
    5. There are substantial transactions costs associated with going private, and the owners may not be able to realize the enhanced value of their shares until the company goes public again, repeating the transactions expenditures.
  D. A leveraged buyout is an ownership transfer consummated primarily with debt.

1. LBO candidates have common characteristics, such as:
   a. there is an opportunity to defer major expenditures for several years,
   b. R&D expenditure requirements are low,
   c. there may be subsidiary assets that can be sold without adversely impacting the core business,
   d. operating cash flows are stable and predictable,
   e. physical assets and/or brand names, but not personnel, are the basis of the business,
   f. the experience and quality of senior management are critical.
2. A leveraged buyout typically involves three types of financing:
   a. a proportionately small equity commitment is made by the existing management of the division,
   b. the majority of the purchase price is borrowed in the form of senior, secured debt, at floating rates,
   c. the balance of the purchase price comes from junior subordinated debt (rated as junk bonds).
3. Empirical studies have found that:
   a. stockholders typically receive a sizable premium when their stock is bought out,
   b. operating performance, cash flows, and the productivity of capital improve after the buyout,
   c. small wealth transfers exist between pre-buyout bondholders and post-buyout stockholders.
4. The long-run viability of an LBO is diminished by the emphasis on short-term cash flow and profitability, arising from the two kinds of risk specific to LBOs:
   a. business risk involves the possibility that operations may not go according to plan, and the cash flow may be less than forecasted, to the point where debt obligations cannot be met.
   b. financial risk involves the high and floating interest charges and huge debt-repayment schedules that must be met.
E. A leveraged recapitalization (or leveraged cash out) occurs when a publicly traded company raises cash through massive leverage and distributes it to stockholders as a huge dividend.
   1. The stock (known as "stub" shares) continues to trade publicly, but at a much lower price.
   2. Management and other insiders do not participate in the payout but take additional shares instead.
   3. Leveraged recaps occur in response to a hostile takeover threat or to management's perception that the company is vulnerable to such a threat.
   4. Empirical studies have found excess returns at about the same general level as for LBOs.

MULTIPLE CHOICE QUESTIONS

25.1 The reason cited must frequently for an involuntary divestiture is
a. increased cash flow.
b. reduced risk.
c. strategic realignment.
d. government requirements.

25.2 Which of the following is not a motive for voluntary divestitures?
a. efficiency gains
b. wealth transfers
c. tax reasons
d. diversification

25.3 The disposal of an entire company or of some business unit to another firm is a
a. sell-off.
b. spin-off.
c. equity carveout.
d. leveraged buyout.

25.4 The divestiture most like a reverse merger is a
a. sell-off.
b. spin-off.
c. equity carveout.
d. leveraged buyout.

25.5 Which of the following reasons cited as justifying a spin-off is not supported by empirical evidence?
a. contractual flexibility
b. management efficiency
c. wealth transfer
d. information effect

25.6 In an equity carveout, voting control of the new firm rests with the
a. old company.
b. management of the business unit that forms the new firm.
c. new stockholders.
d. government.

25.7 Motivations for going private include all the following except
a. elimination of the need for annual public meetings.
b. management may be better able to concentrate on a long-term perspective.
c. management has an incentive to work more efficiently.
d. liquidity is improved.

25.8 Junk bonds arise from
   a. sell-offs.
   b. spin-offs.
   c. leveraged buyouts.
   d. equity carveouts.

25.9 The greatest disadvantage of leveraged buyouts is
   a. limited potential return.
   b. high risk.
   c. concentration on long-term aspects.
   d. little subordinated debt.

25.10 The difference between a leveraged buyout (LBO) and a leveraged cashout (LCO) is
   a. in a LCO, the public keeps its stock.
   b. in a LBO, the public keeps its stock.
   c. in a LCO, the insiders provide their own personal debt.
   d. in a LBO, the insiders provide their own personal debt.

ANSWERS

25.1	d	p.	667		25.6	b	pp.	672-673
25.2	d	p.	667		25.7	d	pp.	673-674
25.3	a	p.	669		25.8	c	p.	676
25.4	b	p.	671		25.9	b	p.	678
25.5	c	p.	672		25.10	a	p.	679

CHAPTER 26

INTERNATIONAL FINANCIAL MANAGEMENT

PERSPECTIVE

International investment and capital raising combined with the globalization of financial institutions and instruments have changed the environment of the financial manager.

Capital budgeting requires estimates of future cash flows, future exchange rates, international inflation rates, and consideration of tax differences and political risks.

Changes in foreign exchange rates expose a company to three types of risk in its foreign operations: translation exposure refers to the effects of such changes on the company's financial statements; transaction exposure refers to the effects of such changes on a particular transaction; and economic exposure refers to the impact of these changes on the economic value of the firm.

Management of exchange-rate exposure can be done in many ways. Advantage can be taken of natural hedges. Multinational firms can balance monetary assets and liabilities and adjust intercompany accounts. Any company can hedge by financing in different currencies, using commercial banks, trade drafts, Eurodollar loans and deposits, and international bonds. Finally, there are currency hedges, which include forward contracts, futures contracts, currency options, and currency swaps.

Inflation, interest rates, and exchange rates are theoretically related through the concepts of purchasing power parity and interest rate parity. Empirical evidence supports this theory in the long run, but not in the short run.

International trade is facilitated by standardized procedures which involve three specific documents; a draft, a bill of lading, and a letter of credit.

CHAPTER OUTLINE

I. Investing capital in a foreign operation, whether in pursuit of markets, production facilities, and/or raw materials, must be consistent with the objective of securing a higher rate of return than is possible in a domestic operation.
   A. The calculations for international capital budgeting are the same as for domestic capital budgeting, but additional factors must be considered.
      1. The relevant cash inflows for a foreign investment are those that can be repatriated to the parent.

2. Foreign cash flows must be translated into their U.S. dollar equivalents at the expected exchange rate.
   B. Foreign investments may reduce risk to the extent that returns on investment projects tend to be less correlated among countries than they are in any one particular country.
      1. If capital markets were perfect, investors could effectively replicate any asset diversification by the firm, and foreign investment would not enhance shareholder wealth.
      2. Capital markets are imperfect because of currency restrictions, investment barriers, legal restrictions, lack of information, differences in taxation, and different degrees of political risk exist.
   C. Different tax laws and different tax treatments of foreign investment complicate international operations.
      1. If a U.S. corporation carries on business abroad through a branch or division, the income from that operation is reported on the company's U.S. tax form and is taxed in the same way as domestic income.
      2. Unlike dividends from a domestic corporation, dividends received by a U.S. corporation from a foreign subsidiary are fully taxable.
      3. Every country taxes income of foreign companies doing business in that country, but the amount and type of tax varies:
         a. Some countries impose a lower tax on income distributed to stockholders than on retained earnings.
         b. Less-developed countries frequently provide tax incentives to encourage foreign investment.
         c. European countries have a value-added tax, in essence a sales tax on each stage of production.
         d. The definition of what constitutes taxable income is different for different countries.
      4. To avoid double taxation, the U.S. gives a federal income tax credit for foreign taxes paid by a U.S. corporation.
      5. From time to time, various special U.S. tax incentives come into existence to help export industries.
   D. A multinational company faces political risks ranging from mild interference to complete confiscation of all assets.
      1. Political instability is another element in the capital budgeting decision that must be forecasted.
      2. Once a company decides to invest, it may find a joint venture beneficial or even necessary.

II. A company with foreign operations is exposed to risk emanating from changes in exchange rates.
   A. The spot exchange rate is the current price of one currency relative to another; the forward exchange rate is the

future price of one currency relative to another, as forecasted today.

B. Translation exposure to foreign exchange risk is the change in accounting income and balance sheet statements caused by changes in exchange rates.

1. A U.S. company must determine a functional currency for each of its foreign subsidiaries: either the local currency or the dollar. (If the local currency inflates at more than 100 percent per annum, the dollar must be used.)

2. If the local currency is the functional currency, all assets and liabilities are translated at the current rate of exchange and translation gains or losses affect the owners' equity instead of the income statement.

3. If the dollar is the functional currency, then:

a. Cash, receivables, liabilities, sales, expenses, and taxes are translated using current exchange rates.

b. Inventories, plant and equipment, equity, cost of goods sold, and depreciation are translated at the historical exchange rates existing at the time of the transactions.

c. The translation gain or loss is added to or subtracted from net income.

C. Transactions exposure to foreign exchange risk involves settling a particular transaction at one exchange rate when the obligation was originally recorded at another.

D. Economic exposure to foreign exchange risk involves changes in expected future cash flows caused by a change in exchange rates.

1. Unanticipated changes in exchange rates can affect the value of the company's stock.

2. An exposure coefficient can be created for balance sheet items, such that:

a. if the coefficient is 1.0, then a 10 percent increase in the local currency will cause a 10 percent decrease in the dollar market value of the asset.

b. if the coefficient is 0, then an increase in the local currency will not cause a decrease in the dollar market value of the asset.

3. Monetary assets and liabilities have an exposure coefficient of 1.0; real assets have a coefficient between 0 and 1.0.

4. Exposed market value for balance sheet items is calculated by multiplying the market value of each item by its exposure coefficient.

5. Total asset exposure less total liability exposure equals net aggregate market value exposure.

6. Net aggregate market value exposure divided by the market value of the equity equals the aggregate exposure coefficient.

7. If the local currency should rise by 10 percent and a subsidiary had an aggregate exposure coefficient of 0.21, then the subsidiary's U.S. dollar value would decline by 2.1 percent.
E. There are many ways to manage exchange-rate exposure.
   1. A natural hedge, which makes profit margins insensitive to changes in exchange rates, is created when:
      a. a subsidiary's raw materials are obtained in global markets and its finished products are sold in global markets, or
      b. a subsidiary's raw materials are obtained locally and its finished products are sold locally.
   2. Careful cash management can reduce exchange-rate exposure in several ways; if a currency is expected to depreciate in value:
      a. Cash should be reduced to a minimum by the purchase of inventories or other real assets.
      b. Accounts receivable should be kept as fresh as possible, and the extension of trade credit should be minimized.
      c. Accounts payable should be stretched as far as possible.
      d. Local currency loans should replace advances made by the U.S. parent.
      e. Expected appreciation in the local currency should be managed by reversing the above steps.
   3. A multinational company can protect itself from foreign exchange risks by:
      a. adjusting transfer of funds commitments between countries,
      b. adjusting intercompany dividends and royalty payments,
      c. varying transfer pricing of components or of finished goods to the extent allowed by law.
   4. If a company's assets are exposed in one currency, it can borrow in that country to offset the exposure; there are a wide variety of sources of external financing available.
      a. Foreign merchant banks and international branches of U.S. commercial banks perform essentially the same financing function as domestic banks do in the U.S.
      b. The Eurodollar market is a major source of short-term financing for the working capital requirements of the multinational company, and many American firms arrange for lines of credit and revolving credits from Eurodollar banks.
      c. Eurobonds are denominated in a single currency but traded over the counter in many countries; foreign bonds are issued by a foreign government or corporation in a local market; Yankee bonds are issued by non-Americans in the U.S. market; "samurai" bonds are issued by non-Japanese in the

Japanese market, and floating-rate notes often involve multiple currencies.
    d. Certain bonds provide the holder with the right to choose the currency in which payment is received, prior to each coupon or principal payment. The exchange rate is fixed at the time of issue.
    e. An instrument denominated in one currency may have a conversion option which allows it to be converted into a different instrument denominated in another currency. The conversion ratio and the exchange rate are set at the time the security is issued.
    f. Dual currency bonds pay interest and principal in different currencies.
  5. Currency exposure can be hedged through any one of several currency markets.
    a. In the forward exchange market, one buys a forward contract for the exchange of one currency for another at a specific future date and at a specific exchange ratio.
    b. A currency futures contract is a standardized agreement that calls for delivery of one of the eight major currencies at some specified future date, and is marked to market each day.
    c. Currency options contracts (puts and calls) give the holder the right, but not the obligation, to buy or sell the currency over the life of the contract. There are options on both spot market currencies and on currency futures contracts.
    d. In a currency swap, two parties exchange debt obligations denominated in different currencies. Each agrees to pay the other's interest obligation. At maturity, principal amounts are exchanged, usually at a rate of exchange agreed upon in advance.
    e. With a combined currency/interest-rate swap, there is an exchange of fixed-rate for floating-rate payments where the two payments are in different currencies. A number of extensions are possible: more than two currencies, options, and other features.
  6. Large multinationals engage in self-insurance, based on the notion that changes in exchange rates average out over time with enough commercial transactions.
  7. The costs of bankruptcy and agency costs make extensive exposure unwise for the smaller firm, and they should manage their currency-risk exposure.

III. In the long run, there is correlation between domestic and foreign inflation, and between interest rates and foreign exchange rates; in the short run, fluctuations in exchange rates are continual and often defy explanation.

A. The law of one price says that a commodity will sell for the same price, regardless of where it is purchased.
  1. This assumes that transportation and transactions costs are zero.
  2. It also assumes there are no impediments to trade.
B. Purchasing power parity (PPP) says that the rate of exchange between currencies of two countries is directly related to the differential rate of inflation between them.
  1. How closely a country's exchange rate corresponds to purchasing power parity depends on the price elasticity of exports and imports.
  2. Products in mature industries generally conform more closely to PPP than products in newer industries with emerging technology.
  3. PPP does not work well when a country intervenes in the exchange-rate market.
C. Interest rate parity (IRP) says that if interest rates are higher in one country than they are in another, the former's currency will sell at a discount in the forward market.
  1. The international Fisher effect suggests that differences in interest rates between two countries serve as a proxy for differences in expected inflation.
  2. If IRP did not occur, covered interest arbitrage would reduce the interest rate differential and the discount on the forward exchange rate until IRP were established and arbitrage actions had zero profit potential.
  3. Interest-rate differentials are a proxy for forward exchange rate/spot exchange rate differentials, and vice versa.
D. Empirically, neither PPP nor IRP hold in the short run, because there are too many market imperfections for international equilibrium to be achieved.
E. Empirically, both PPP and IRP hold in the long run.

IV. Foreign trade differs from domestic trade with respect to the instruments and documents employed.
  A. Most domestic sales are on open-account credit; procedures for international trade require 3 key documents:
    1. The international draft ("trade draft," "bill of exchange") is simply a written statement by the exporter ordering the importer to pay a specific amount of money at a specific time.
      a. A sight draft is payable on presentation to the party to whom the draft is addressed; a time draft is payable a given number of days after sight.
      b. The draft is unconditional.
      c. Upon presentation of a time draft, it is accepted by either the drawee or his bank; if the bank is large and well known, this "banker's acceptance" becomes a marketable security for the remainder of its time outstanding.

185

2. A bill of lading is a shipping document used in the transportation of goods from the exporter to the importer and has several functions:
   a. It serves as a receipt from the transportation company to the exporter.
   b. It serves as a contract between the transportation company and the exporter to ship the goods and deliver them to a specific party at a specific destination.
   c. It can serve as a document of title for the holder.
3. A commercial letter of credit is issued by a bank on behalf of the importer, which agrees to honor a draft drawn on the importer, provided the bill of lading and other details are in order.
   a. In essence, the bank substitutes its credit for that of the importer.
   b. A bank in the exporter's country may confirm the letter of credit, obligating itself to honor drafts drawn in keeping with the letter of credit arrangement.
   c. The letter itself can be either irrevocable or revocable, but drafts drawn under an irrevocable letter must be honored by the issuing bank.

MULTIPLE CHOICE QUESTIONS

26.1 Which of the following is not peculiar to foreign investment?
   a. exchange-rate risk
   b. political risk
   c. business risk
   d. inability to repatriate earnings

26.2 Dividends of a foreign subsidiary paid to a U.S. firm are
   a. exempt from taxes.
   b. 50% exempt from taxes.
   c. 70% exempt from taxes.
   d. taxed as ordinary income.

26.3 In order to avoid double taxation,
   a. foreign dividends are exempt from U.S. taxes.
   b. an unlimited credit is granted for taxes paid foreign governments.
   c. a limited credit is granted for taxes paid foreign governments.
   d. the U.S. uses a value added tax in place of income taxes on foreign profits.

26.4 The most severe political risk is
a. inability to repatriate earnings.
b. expropriation.
c. restriction on convertibility of currencies.
d. required investment in social projects.

26.5 The rate of exchange used to translate financial statements of foreign subsidiaries is determined by the
a. management of the firm.
b. functional currency used.
c. internal revenue service.
d. foreign accounting convention.

26.6 A natural hedge occurs when a foreign subsidiary buys raw materials whose prices are determined _____ and sells its products at prices which are determined _____.
a. in global markets, in global markets
b. in global markets, domestically
c. domestically, in global markets
d. in the U.S., domestically

26.7 If a firm believes that the value of the currency of a country is going to drop sharply, it should
a. simultaneously borrow and lend in that currency.
b. borrow in that currency.
c. lend in that currency.
d. pay off debt in that currency.

26.8 If a German subsidiary of an American company issued a bond that was denominated in Deutschemarks and traded all over Europe, that bond would be called a
a. Yankee bond.
b. foreign bond.
c. Eurobond.
d. currency cocktail bond.

26.9 Whether or not a firm gains by using the forward exchange market to protect itself against exchange rate fluctuations is dependent upon the
a. current and future spot rate.
b. current spot rate and future forward rate.
c. current forward rate and the current spot rate.
d. current forward rate and the future spot rate.

26.10 The document which often serves as a document of title is
a. the letter of credit.
b. the bill of lading.
c. the trade draft.
d. the trade acceptance.

ANSWERS

26.1 c pp. 686-689   26.6   a p. 697
26.2 d p.   688   26.7   b p. 698
26.3 c p.   688   26.8   c p. 700
26.4 b p.   689   26.9   d p. 702
26.5 b p.   691   26.10 b p. 714

CHAPTER 27

FINANCIAL RATIO ANALYSIS

PERSPECTIVE

Financial ratios derived from the balance sheet and income statement are used by creditors, investors, and government regulators to establish creditworthiness, investment potential, or conformity with legal limitations. They are also helpful internally for management control.

The ratios measure four things: liquidity, debt, profitability, and coverage of fixed charges. They can be evaluated for one company over time, or for a whole industry at a point in time.

Ratios can be used with varying degrees of success to predict bond ratings, stock prices, and bankruptcy.

Financial statements can be common sized, meaning that balance sheets can be restated as a percentage of total assets and income statements restated as a percentage of sales. Alternatively, both statements can be indexed to statements from some base year. Reworking the statements in this way is helpful in identifying trends over time.

CHAPTER OUTLINE

I. Financial analysis is done internally by a company's management and externally by creditors, investors, and government regulators for various purposes.
   A. The analysis of a company's financial statements using ratios can be done in two ways:
      1. The analyst can compare a present ratio with past and expected future ratios for the same company, in order to evaluate any trend that may exist.
      2. The analyst may compare the ratios of one firm with those of similar firms or with industry averages at the same point in time, in order to evaluate relative condition and performance. Industry ratios are available from:
         a. Dun and Bradstreet,
         b. Robert Morris Associates,
         c. Prentice Hall,
         d. the FTC and SEC jointly,
         e. various credit agencies and trade associations.
   B. The interpretation of ratios and comparisons thereof can be misleading if not done carefully.

189

1. It helps to have information on the dispersion of a particular ratio throughout the industry, as well as the industry average.
2. The financial condition and performance of an industry may be less than satisfactory, so a company's being "above average" is not necessarily wonderful.
3. The company and the industry may not be strictly comparable because the industry may not be homogeneous or the company may have multiple product lines.
4. Companies should be compared with companies of like size.
5. Accounting practices are not as standardized as the standardized financial statements would suggest.

II. Financial ratios can be grouped according to type.
   A. Liquidity ratios are used to judge a firm's ability to meet short-term obligations and to remain solvent in the event of adversities.
      1. Current Ratio = Current Assets / Current Liabilities. The higher the ratio, the greater the ability of the firm to pay its bills. But the ratio does not take into account the liquidity of the individual components of the current assets.
      2. Acid-Test/Quick Ratio = (Current Assets - Inventories) / Current Liabilities. The higher the ratio, the greater the ability of the firm to pay its bills. The ratio uses only the most liquid of the current assets--cash, marketable securities, and receivables.
      3. Average Collection Period = (Receivables)(365)/ Annual Credit Sales. The smaller this ratio, the greater the ability of the firm to pay its bills. If the period is large when compared to the terms of trade being offered by the company, a sizable portion of receivables may be past due and/or uncollectible.
      4. Receivable Turnover Ratio = Annual Credit Sales / Receivables. The larger this ratio, the greater the ability of the firm to pay its bills. This is the reciprocal of the average collection period, and can be alternatively calculated as: Receivable Turnover Ratio = 365 / Average Collection Period.
      5. Internally, the receivables ratios can be supplemented with an Aging of Accounts Schedule, which examines the distribution of receivables relative to how long they have been outstanding, and with a Conversion Matrix of Receivables into Cash, which separates changes in the payment behavior of customers from changes in the pattern of sales.

190

6. Average Payable Period = (Payables)(365)/ Purchases.
   The smaller this ratio, the better the history of the firm in paying its bills. If the period is large when compared to the terms of trade be offered to the company, it may be experiencing serious cash flow problems.
7. It is also possible to calculate a Payable Turnover Ratio, an Aging of Accounts Schedule, and a Conversion Matrix of Payables. Information for these analyses is usually only available internally, although the data would be valuable in estimating the probability that a credit applicant will pay on time.
8. Inventory Turnover Ratio = Cost of Goods Sold/ Average Inventory.
   The higher the ratio, the more efficient the inventory management of a firm. But a ratio that is too high may indicate too little inventory and frequent stockouts. A very low ratio may indicate that a company has a lot of obsolete inventory, which will necessitate significant writedowns in the future.

B. Debt ratios measure the ability of a firm to meet its long-term obligations.
1. Debt to Net Worth Ratio = Total Debt / Shareholders' Equity.
   The higher the ratio, the greater the financial risk of the company.
2. Debt to Capitalization Ratio = Long Term Debt / (Long Term Debt + Shareholders' Equity).
   The higher the ratio, the greater the relative importance of long-term debt in the company's capital structure, and the greater the financial risk.
3. Cash Flow to Total Liabilities Ratio = EBITD / Total Liabilities.
   Cash flow is defined as earnings before interest, taxes and depreciation (EBITD).
   The higher this ratio, the greater the ability of a company to service its debt.
4. Cash Flow to Long Term Debt Ratio = EBITD / Long Term Debt.
   The higher this ratio, the greater the ability of a company to service its bonds.
5. Total Interest-Bearing Debt plus Equity to Operating Cash Flows Ratio = (Total Borrowings + Equity)/EBITD
   This is particularly helpful in corporate restructuring. Lenders in highly levered transactions become concerned when the ratio exceeds 8, as the possibility of default has been found to be significant at this point.

C. Coverage ratios relate the financial charges of a firm to its ability to service them.

1. Overall Interest Coverage Ratio = EBIT/ Total Interest
   The higher this ratio, the better the company's ability to service its debt.
2. Cash Flow Coverage Ratio = (EBIT + Gross Depreciation) / (Interest + Gross Principal Payments)
   The variables labeled "Gross" are cash flows that have to be multiplied by [1 / (1 - t)] to correspond to EBIT and interest payments, which are on a before-tax basis. Interest and principal payments are both obligations that have to be met out of cash.

D. Profitability ratios, which relate profits to sales or to investment, indicate the firm's efficiency of operation.
   1. Gross Profit Margin = (Sales - Cost of Goods Sold) / Sales
      This indicates the efficiency of operations as well as how products are priced.
   2. Net Profit Margin = Net Profits after Taxes / Sales.
      This indicates the efficiency of the firm after taking into account operations, financing, and taxes, but not extraordinary charges.
      If the Gross Profit Margin is stable over time but the Net Profit Margin falls, either financing expenses or taxes have increased.
   3. Rate of Return on Equity (ROE) = (Net Profit after Taxes - Preferred Dividend) / Shareholders' Equity.
      This ratio indicates the earning power on shareholders' book investment and is frequently used in comparing two or more firms.
      If market value is used in the denominator, the ratio becomes the Earnings/Price Ratio of the stock.
   4. Return on Assets (ROA) = Net Profit after Taxes / Total Assets.
      This is a more general ratio indicating the earning power of the company's investment in assets.
   5. Net Operating Profit Rate of Return = EBIT / Total Assets.
      This ratio is preferable to ROA when a company's financial charges are significant, because the creditors provide means by which part of the total assets are supported.
      This ratio is independent of the way assets are financed.
   6. Asset Turnover Ratio = Sales / Total Assets.
      This ratio tells us the relative efficiency with which the firm utilizes its resources in order to generate output. The industry standard is highly significant.
   7. Earning Power = Net Profit after Taxes / Total Assets.
      This ratio can be constructed another way:
      Earning Power = (Asset Turnover)(Net Profit Margin).
      This ratio ignores neither the utilization of assets nor the profitability on sales.

III. Selected ratios are used by different interested parties for predictive purposes.
  A. An investor might feel that the Return on Investment Ratio and the various Profit Margin Ratios would be the best for predicting the future value of a stock.
  B. Empirical studies have been successful in predicting the long-term credit standing of a firm by using:
    1. debt-to-equity ratios,
    2. cash-flow-to-debt ratios,
    3. net operating profit margins,
    4. debt coverage and its stability,
    5. return on investment,
    6. size,
    7. earnings stability.
  C. A multiple discriminant analysis to predict bankruptcies up to 2 years before they happened was successful using:
    1. working capital to total assets,
    2. cumulative retained earnings to total assets,
    3. EBIT to total assets,
    4. market value of equity to book value of total debt,
    5. sales to total assets.
  D. A more recent multiple discriminant analysis to predict bankruptcies up to 5 years before they happened was successful using:
    1. return on assets ratio,
    2. stability of earnings,
    3. interest coverage ratio,
    4. retained earnings to total assets ratio,
    5. current ratio,
    6. common equity to total capital ratio,
    7. size of total assets.

IV. Restating the financial statements can produce insights into underlying improvement or deterioration of performance over time.
  A. Common size analysis expresses all items on the balance sheet as a percent of total assets and all items on the income statement as a percent of sales.
  B. Index analysis expresses all financial statement items as an index relative to some base year.

APPENDIX
  Financial analysts may wish to differentiate performance attributable to management decisions from profitability attributable to inflation.
  A. Historical cost accounting data are distorted from year to year as a result of inflation.
  B. Financial ratios, particularly those measuring profitability, are overstated as a result of inflation.
  C. Interindustry comparisons can also be distorted over time: a company with older fixed assets will show a higher ROI in an inflationary environment than will a company with newer

fixed assets. The former company may be much less efficient in an economic sense, but this will not be apparent in the ratios unless the effects of inflation are factored in.

MULTIPLE CHOICE QUESTIONS

27.1 Trade creditors are most interested in
a. liquidity ratios.
b. debt ratios.
c. coverage ratios.
d. profitability ratios.

27.2 Equity investors and potential equity investors are most likely to concentrate on
a. liquidity ratios.
b. debt ratios.
c. coverage ratios.
d. profitability ratios.

27.3 Sources of industry data include ratios published by all of the following except
a. the firm itself.
b. Robert Morris Associates.
c. Dun and Bradstreet.
d. trade associations.

27.4 Most published financial ratios are based on
a. market values.
b. liquidation values.
c. present values.
d. book values.

27.5 If a significant portion of a company's receivables are past due, an analyst would expect
a. the average collection period to be short and growing shorter as time passes.
b. the receivable turnover ratio to be high and growing higher as time passes.
c. the average collection period to be longer than the net period in the terms of trade extended by the company.
d. the conversion matrix of credit sales to cash to be uniform.

27.6 A low inventory turnover would typically be associated with
a. little obsolescence in the inventory.
b. few inventory write-downs.
c. efficient handling of inventory.
d. a high level of inventory.

27.7 Which of the following ratios is affected by the way in which the firm is financed?
   a. inventory turnover
   b. asset turnover
   c. gross profit margin
   d. net profit margin

27.8 Return on assets (ROA) can be calculated by
   a. multiplying return on equity by owners' equity.
   b. multiplying net profit margin by the asset turnover.
   c. multiplying the gross margin by assets.
   d. dividing the ROE by the asset turnover.

27.9 On the basis of empirical studies, it appears that with regard to the credit standing of a firm,
   a. ratio analysis is useless.
   b. a handful of ratios can be used successfully.
   c. it takes a dozen or more ratios to have any success.
   d. to get the best results, it takes more than 20 ratios.

27.10 In a period of inflation, the rate of return on assets will be higher for an older firm than for a new firm because the older one has
   a. higher profit and higher assets.
   b. lower profit and higher assets.
   c. higher profit and lower assets.
   d. lower assets and lower profit.

ANSWERS

27.1	a	p.	724		27.6	d	p.	733
27.2	d	p.	724		27.7	d	p.	737
27.3	a	p.	725		27.8	b	p.	738
27.4	d	p.	726		27.9	b	p.	740
27.5	c	p.	730		27.10	c	p.	750

CHAPTER 28

FINANCIAL PLANNING

███████████████████████████████████

PERSPECTIVE

This chapter examines four analytical tools available to the financial manager.

Sources and uses of funds statements help in analyzing the commitment of funds to assets and in planning the company's financing.

Cash budgets, which are forecasts of cash receipts and disbursements, allow the financial manager to plan investments in marketable securities and to make arrangements to meet expected borrowing needs. Alternate cash budgets allow analysis of a range of possible cash positions.

The preparation of pro forma income statements and balance sheets gives a financial manager insight into the expected financial condition and performance of the company.

Sustainable growth modeling is a powerful tool for checking the consistency between sales growth goals, operating efficiency, and financial objectives.

CHAPTER OUTLINE

I. Financial planning involves analyzing the past, present, and future financial flows of a company, to determine the most likely course of events and possible deviations from it.
   A. A sources and uses of funds statement shows the net changes in each over a period of time, as determined by comparing the differences in two balance sheets and two income statements.
      1. Sources of funds that increase cash are:
         a. a net decrease in any asset other than cash or fixed assets,
         b. a gross decrease in fixed assets,
         c. a net increase in any liability,
         d. proceeds from the sale of preferred or common stock,
         e. funds provided by operations.
      2. Uses of funds that decrease cash are:
         a. a net increase in any asset other than cash or fixed assets,
         b. a gross increase in fixed assets,
         c. a net decrease in any liability,

           d. a retirement or purchase of stock,

           e. cash dividends.

      3. When total uses are subtracted from total sources, the difference should equal the actual change in cash between the two statement dates.

  B. An accounting statement of cash flows is also derived from a comparison of balance sheets and income statements, but there are a few differences in presentation.

      1. Sources of cash are shown as positive numbers; uses of cash are negative numbers. All appear in a single column.

      2. The statement is categorized into operating activities, investing activities, and financing activities.

      3. The statement records not only gross investment in fixed assets, but also dispositions.

      4. The final reconciliation, the change in cash position, is the same.

  C. A sources and uses of working capital statement takes into account working capital instead of cash.

      1. It omits changes in the various components of current assets and current liabilities.

      2. It is frequently used by bankers and other lenders.

      3. Management can use it for internal control.

  D. Analysis of flow of funds statements may serve several purposes.

      1. An analysis of several years may point out disproportionate changes in one or more areas.

      2. The firm's financing can be examined to ensure the appropriate balances of internal vs. external funds, and long-term vs. short-term funds.

      3. An analysis of a projected flow of funds statement is an extremely valuable tool for planning and control.

II. A cash budget is a projection of the timing and amount of expected cash inflows and outflows to determine the future cash needs of the firm.

  A. For most firms, cash inflows result primarily from sales.

      1. The accuracy of the sales forecast is crucial to the accuracy of the cash budget.

          a. An internal forecast of sales can be developed through the marketing department.

          b. An external forecast can be obtained by correlation and extrapolation of economic, industry, and company trends.

          c. Differences between the two forecasts must be reconciled.

      2. Given the sales forecast, the timing and amount of cash receipts from these sales must be projected. This involves consideration of

          a. the terms of trade,

          b. the credit and collection policies,

          c. seasonal patterns.

3. Other sources of cash, such as the sale of assets and interest and dividend income must be included in the cash inflows.

B. The next step in building a cash budget is to predict cash outflows.

1. A production schedule may be tied to sales or stabilized for efficiency.

2. Given a production schedule, estimates can be made of the needs in materials, labor, and additional fixed assets.

3. The expected timing and amounts of cash required to meet these needs are entered in the cash budget.

4. Other cash outflows such as dividends, taxes, repayment of debt or repurchase of stock must be included.

C. When the budget contains all foreseeable cash inflows and outflows, the net cash flow for each month is calculated.

D. These net cash flows are then added to the cash position at the beginning of the budget to get a month-by-month projected cash position.

1. Management can plan to invest excess cash in marketable securities.

2. Borrowing arrangements can be set up to meet anticipated cash deficits.

E. It is desirable to work out additional cash budgets based on alternate sets of assumptions (possibly best-case and worst-case scenarios).

F. Knowledge of possible deviations enables the financial manager to determine more accurately the minimum cash balance, maturity structure of debt, and borrowing power necessary to give the firm a margin of safety.

III. It is often useful to prepare projected ("pro forma") balance sheets and income statements for selected future dates.

A. Much of the information that goes into the preparation of the cash budget can be used to derive pro forma statements.

B. Alternatively, all the items on the statements can be estimated directly.

C. Another approach is to estimate a sales level and then use historical ratios (with or without modifications) to calculate the other statement items.

D. Cash and notes payable are the balancing factors in the preparation of pro forma balance sheets.

IV. The sustainable growth rate (SGR) is the maximum annual percentage increase in sales that can be achieved based on target operating, debt, and dividend payout ratios.

A. The assumptions needed to derive the SGR are:

1. The future is exactly like the past with respect to balance sheet and performance ratios.

2. Equity is increased only through earnings retention.

B. An increase in assets must equal the increase in liabilities and shareholders' equity. This can be expressed as:
$$\Delta S(A/S) = b(NP/S)(S_0 + \Delta S) + [b(NP/S)(S_0 + \Delta S)](D/Eq)$$
where:

A/S = total assets to sales ratio,
NP/S = net profit margin,
b = retention rate of earnings,
D/Eq = debt to equity ratio,
S_0 = most recent annual sales,
ΔS = absolute change in sales from S_0,

and where:

$\Delta S(A/S)$ = increase in assets,
$b(NP/S)(S_0 + \Delta S)$ = increase in retained earnings,
$b(NP/S)(S_0 + \Delta S)(D/Eq)$ = increase in debt.

C. This model can be rearranged as
$$SGR = \Delta S/S = \{b(NP/S)(1 + [D/EQ])\} / \{(A/S) - [b(NP/S)(1 + [D/Eq])]\}.$$

D. The initial assumptions can be relaxed and the model modified to allow for external equity financing and a given dollar amount of dividends (instead of a given retention rate).

E. It is possible to use the model to set a target growth rate of sales and then solve for any one variable on the right-hand side of the equation.
   1. This answers the question, "What level of X is consistent with a growth in sales of, say, 20 percent?"
   2. It is also possible to enter target values for all but one variable in the equation, and then solve for that one variable. This uses the equation as a simulation model.

F. Often in corporate planning, the company wants a number of good things: high sales growth, manufacturing flexibility, moderate use of debt, and high dividends.
   1. These things may be inconsistent with one another.
   2. Sustainable growth modeling enables management to check for such inconsistencies.

MULTIPLE CHOICE QUESTIONS

28.1 Which of the following is not a source of funds?
   a. increases in long-term debt
   b. increases in common stock
   c. decreases in inventory
   d. decreases in notes payable

28.2 If funds are defined as working capital, which of the following is not a use of funds?
   a. payment of dividends
   b. purchase of fixed assets
   c. repayment of debt
   d. purchase of marketable securities

28.3 The most important step in developing a cash budget is
a. determining the payroll.
b. estimating sales.
c. estimating income taxes.
d. determining the payments on account.

28.4 Which of the following would not be included in the cash budget?
a. collections of receivables
b. income tax payments
c. depreciation
d. sale of marketable securities

28.5 Which of the following statements is not true?
a. A cash budget can be made for almost any period of time.
b. The cash budget is only as useful as the accuracy of the forecasts that are used to prepare it.
c. The amount of cash cushion a firm should maintain is negatively related to the uncertainty of the cash flows.
d. The purpose of the cash budget is to enable the financial manager to determine and plan for the financing needs of the firm.

28.6 In the cash budgeting context, a cash deficit means
a. cash is less than zero.
b. the firm goes bankrupt.
c. cash is less than the minimum target cash balance.
d. dividends must be postponed.

28.7 One way to develop pro forma statements is to use information accumulated during the building of a cash budget. Which of the following items cannot be transferred from the cash budget to the pro forma statements?
a. cash
b. inventory
c. sales
d. interest

28.8 Sustainable growth is not based on a target
a. current ratio.
b. profit margin.
c. debt ratio.
d. dividend payout.

28.9 The measure of operating efficiency in the sustainable growth model is
a. assets-to-sales.
b. the debt-equity ratio.
c. the dividend payout ratio.
d. change in sales from one period to another.

28.10 Which of the following does not result in an increase in the sustainable growth rate?
 a. reduction in the asset-to-sales ratio
 b. decrease in the dividend payout ratio
 c. sale of common stock
 d. decrease in the debt-equity ratio

ANSWERS

28.1	d	p.	765		28.6	c	p.	774
28.2	d	p.	768		28.7	b	pp.	776-777
28.3	b	p.	770		28.8	a	p.	781
28.4	c	p.	773		28.9	a	p.	781
28.5	c	pp.	774-775		28.10	d	p.	785

APPENDIX A

REMEDIES FOR A FAILING COMPANY

I. A company in financial difficulty can settle matters with its creditors voluntarily.
  A. An extension involves creditors postponing the maturity of their obligations.
    1. All creditors must agree to the extension.
    2. The major creditors usually form a committee to negotiate satisfactory terms with the company.
  B. A composition involves a pro rata settlement of creditors' claims in cash or in cash and promissory notes, but all creditors must agree to accept this partial settlement in discharge of their entire claim.
  C. Voluntary liquidations avoid the costs of bankruptcy court, but again, all creditors must agree to accept whatever settlement can be made.

II. A failing company can be either rehabilitated or liquidated in bankruptcy court.
  A. A voluntary court proceeding begins when the debtor files a petition; it provides immediate protection from creditors.
  B. An involuntary court proceeding begins when 3 or more unsecured creditors with claims of at least $5,000 file a petition; the court issues an order of relief pending a more permanent solution.
  C. Liquidation under Chapter 7 of the Bankruptcy Law involves
    1. the proving of claims against the debtor,
    2. the appointment of a trustee who is responsible for liquidating the property of the company,
    3. the distribution of liquidating dividends to creditors according to the priority of their claims,
    4. discharge of the debtor with relief from any further claims.
  D. Reorganization under Chapter 11 of the Bankruptcy Law is an effort to keep a company alive by changing its capital structure.
    1. In most cases, the debtor continues to run the business, but a trustee can assume operating responsibility for a company.
    2. A fair, equitable, and feasible reorganization plan must be drawn up and filed within 120 days.

3. More than one-half in number and two-thirds in amount of total claims in each claimholder class must vote in favor of the plan if it is to be accepted.
4. If it is rejected, the court imposes a plan on all claimholders.
5. The debtor and all creditors and stockholders are bound by an accepted or imposed plan.

III. A reorganization plan involves the reduction of fixed charges by substituting equity and limited-income securities for fixed-income securities. It is formulated in 3 steps:
A. The total value of the reorganized company is determined by capitalizing expected earnings.
B. A new capital structure for the company is formulated to reduce fixed charges by
1. scaling down the debt by partially shifting it to income bonds, preferred stock, and common stock,
2. extending the maturity of the debt to reduce the annual sinking fund,
3. providing a debt to equity ratio low enough to allow for future financing if needed.
C. The old securities are valued and exchanged for new securities.
1. All senior claims on assets must be settled in full before a junior claim can be settled.
2. The total valuation established in the first step sets an upper limit on the amount of securities that can be issued.
3. Under the rule of absolute priority, it is possible that the common stockholders will get nothing at all.

MULTIPLE CHOICE QUESTIONS

A.1   Which of the following is most likely to be an involuntary settlement?
a. extension
b. composition
c. assignment
d. bankruptcy

A.2   A voluntary settlement in which the creditors agree to take less than the full amount in settlement of their claim is called
a. an extension.
b. a composition.
c. an assignment.
d. lengthening.

A.3   Chapter 7 of the Bankruptcy Law deals with _____ and Chapter
        11 deals with _____.
        a. liquidation, reorganization
        b. reorganization, liquidation
        c. assignment, extension
        d. extension, assignment

A.4   Compared to a private liquidation, the major disadvantage of
        bankruptcy is that
        a. it is more expensive.
        b. it is done more quickly.
        c. it is less equitable.
        d. stockholders get less.

A.5   In a reorganization, the plan should be
        a. fair and include current stockholders.
        b. feasible and include current stockholders.
        c. equitable and feasible.
        d. fair, equitable, and feasible.

A.6   The purpose of establishing a new capital structure for a
        company being reorganized is
        a. to get rid of the old creditors.
        b. to waive the interest owed on the old debt.
        c. to reduce fixed charges to an amount that can **be**
           affordable in the future.
        d. to minimize income taxes.

A.7   Generally, the rule followed in reorganization cases is the
        principle of
        a. relative priority.
        b. absolute priority.
        c. definitive priority.
        d. subordinate priority.

ANSWERS

A.1   d   p.   797
A.2   b   p.   797
A.3   a   p.   798
A.4   a   p.   798
A.5   d   p.   799
A.6   c   p.   800
A.7   b   p.   801

APPENDIX B

MATHEMATICAL TABLES

TABLE A

FUTURE VALUE INTEREST FACTOR OF $1

n	1%	2%	3%	4%	5%	6%	7%	8%
1	1.010	1.020	1.030	1.040	1.050	1.060	1.070	1.080
2	1.020	1.040	1.061	1.082	1.102	1.124	1.145	1.166
3	1.030	1.061	1.093	1.125	1.158	1.191	1.225	1.260
4	1.041	1.082	1.126	1.170	1.216	1.262	1.311	1.360
5	1.051	1.104	1.159	1.217	1.276	1.338	1.403	1.469
6	1.062	1.126	1.194	1.265	1.340	1.419	1.501	1.587
7	1.072	1.149	1.230	1.316	1.407	1.504	1.606	1.714
8	1.083	1.172	1.267	1.369	1.477	1.594	1.718	1.851
9	1.094	1.195	1.305	1.423	1.551	1.689	1.836	1.999
10	1.105	1.219	1.344	1.480	1.629	1.791	1.967	2.159
11	1.116	1.243	1.384	1.539	1.710	1.898	2.105	2.332
12	1.127	1.268	1.426	1.601	1.796	2.012	2.252	2.518
13	1.138	1.294	1.489	1.665	1.886	2.133	2.410	2.720
14	1.149	1.319	1.513	1.732	1.980	2.261	2.579	2.937
15	1.161	1.346	1.558	1.801	2.079	2.397	2.759	3.172
16	1.173	1.373	1.605	1.873	2.183	2.540	2.952	3.426
17	1.184	1.400	1.653	1.948	2.292	2.693	3.159	3.700
18	1.196	1.428	1.702	2.026	2.407	2.854	3.380	3.996
19	1.208	1.457	1.754	2.107	2.527	3.026	3.617	4.316
20	1.220	1.486	1.806	2.191	2.653	3.207	3.870	4.661
25	1.282	1.641	2.094	2.666	3.386	4.292	5.427	6.848

n	9%	10%	11%	12%	13%	14%	15%	16%
1	1.090	1.100	1.110	1.120	1.130	1.140	1.150	1.160
2	1.188	1.210	1.232	1.254	1.277	1.300	1.322	1.346
3	1.295	1.331	1.368	1.405	1.443	1.482	1.521	1.561
4	1.412	1.464	1.518	1.574	1.630	1.689	1.749	1.811
5	1.539	1.611	1.685	1.762	1.842	1.925	2.011	2.100
6	1.677	1.772	1.870	1.974	2.082	2.195	2.313	2.436
7	1.828	1.949	2.076	2.211	2.353	2.502	2.660	2.826
8	1.993	2.144	2.305	2.476	2.658	2.853	3.059	3.278
9	2.172	2.358	2.558	2.773	3.004	3.252	3.518	3.803
10	2.367	2.594	2.839	3.106	3.395	3.707	4.046	4.411
11	2.580	2.853	3.152	3.479	3.836	4.226	4.652	5.117
12	2.813	3.138	3.498	3.896	4.335	4.818	5.350	5.936
13	3.066	3.452	3.883	4.363	4.898	5.492	6.153	6.886
14	3.342	3.797	4.310	4.887	5.535	6.261	7.076	7.988
15	3.642	4.177	4.785	5.474	6.254	7.138	8.137	9.266
16	3.970	4.595	5.311	6.130	7.067	8.137	9.358	10.748
17	4.328	5.054	5.895	6.866	7.986	9.276	10.761	12.468
18	4.717	5.560	6.544	7.690	9.024	10.575	12.375	14.463
19	5.142	6.116	7.263	8.613	10.197	12.056	14.232	16.777
20	5.604	6.727	8.062	9.646	11.523	13.743	16.367	19.461
25	8.623	10.835	13.585	17.000	21.231	26.462	32.919	40.874

TABLE B

FUTURE VALUE INTEREST FACTOR OF AN ANNUITY OF $1

n	1%	2%	3%	4%	5%	6%	7%	8%
1	1.000	1.000	1.000	1.000	1.000	1.000	1.000	1.000
2	2.010	2.020	2.030	2.040	2.050	2.060	2.070	2.080
3	3.030	3.060	3.091	3.122	3.153	3.184	3.215	3.246
4	4.060	4.122	4.184	4.246	4.310	4.375	4.440	4.506
5	5.101	5.204	5.309	5.416	5.526	5.637	5.751	5.867
6	6.152	6.308	6.468	6.633	6.802	6.975	7.153	7.336
7	7.214	7.434	7.662	7.898	8.142	8.394	8.654	8.923
8	8.286	8.583	8.892	9.214	9.549	9.897	10.260	10.637
9	9.369	9.755	10.159	10.583	11.027	11.491	11.978	12.488
10	10.462	10.950	11.464	12.006	12.578	13.181	13.816	14.487
11	11.567	12.169	12.808	13.486	14.207	14.972	15.784	16.645
12	12.683	13.412	14.192	15.026	15.917	16.870	17.888	18.977
13	13.809	14.680	15.618	16.627	17.713	18.882	20.141	21.495
14	14.947	15.974	17.086	18.292	19.599	21.015	22.550	24.215
15	16.097	17.293	18.599	20.024	21.579	23.276	25.129	27.152
16	17.258	18.639	20.157	21.825	23.657	25.673	27.888	30.324
17	18.430	20.012	21.762	23.698	25.840	28.213	30.840	33.750
18	19.615	21.412	23.414	25.645	28.132	30.906	33.999	37.450
19	20.811	22.841	25.117	27.671	30.539	33.760	37.379	41.446
20	22.019	24.297	26.870	29.778	33.066	36.786	40.995	45.762
25	28.243	32.030	36.459	41.646	47.727	54.865	63.249	73.106

n	9%	10%	11%	12%	13%	14%	15%	16%
1	1.000	1.000	1.00	1.000	1.000	1.000	1.000	1.000
2	2.090	2.100	2.110	2.120	2.130	2.140	2.150	2.160
3	3.278	3.310	3.342	3.374	3.407	3.440	3.473	3.506
4	4.573	4.641	4.710	4.779	4.850	4.921	4.993	5.066
5	5.985	6.105	6.228	6.353	6.480	6.610	6.742	6.877
6	7.523	7.716	7.913	8.115	8.323	8.536	8.754	8.977
7	9.200	9.487	9.783	10.089	10.405	10.730	11.067	11.414
8	11.028	11.436	11.859	12.300	12.757	13.233	13.727	14.240
9	13.021	13.579	14.164	14.776	15.416	16.085	16.786	17.519
10	15.193	15.937	16.722	17.549	18.420	19.337	20.304	21.321
11	17.560	18.531	19.561	20.655	21.814	23.045	24.349	25.733
12	20.141	21.384	22.713	24.133	25.650	27.271	29.002	30.850
13	22.953	24.523	26.212	28.029	29.985	32.089	34.352	36.786
14	26.019	27.975	30.095	32.393	34.883	37.581	40.505	43.672
15	29.361	31.772	34.405	37.280	40.417	43.842	47.580	51.660
16	33.003	35.950	39.190	42.753	46.672	50.980	55.717	60.925
17	36.974	40.545	44.501	48.884	53.739	59.118	65.075	71.673
18	41.301	45.599	50.396	55.750	61.725	68.394	75.836	84.141
19	46.018	51.159	56.939	63.440	70.749	78.969	88.212	98.603
20	51.160	57.275	64.203	72.052	80.947	91.025	102.44	115.38
25	84.701	98.347	114.41	135.33	155.62	181.87	212.79	249.21

TABLE C

VALUES OF e^{rn}

rn	e^{rn}	rn	e^{rn}	rn	e^{rn}
.01	1.010050	.46	1.584073	0.91	2.484321
.02	1.020201	.47	1.599993	0.92	2.509288
.03	1.030454	.48	1.616073	0.93	2.534507
.04	1.040810	.49	1.632315	0.94	2.559979
.05	1.051271	.50	1.648720	0.95	2.585708
.06	1.061836	.51	1.665290	0.96	2.611694
.07	1.072508	.52	1.682027	0.97	2.637942
.08	1.083287	.53	1.698931	0.98	2.664454
.09	1.094174	.54	1.716006	0.99	2.691232
.10	1.105170	.55	1.733252	1.00	2.718280
.11	1.116277	.56	1.750671	1.01	2.745599
.12	1.127496	.57	1.768266	1.02	2.773192
.13	1.138828	.58	1.786037	1.03	2.801063
.14	1.150273	.59	1.803987	1.04	2.829215
.15	1.161834	.60	1.822118	1.05	2.857649
.16	1.173510	.61	1.840430	1.06	2.886368
.17	1.185304	.62	1.858927	1.07	2.915377
.18	1.197217	.63	1.877609	1.08	2.944677
.19	1.209249	.64	1.896480	1.09	2.974271
.20	1.221402	.65	1.915539	1.10	3.004163
.21	1.233677	.66	1.934791	1.11	3.034356
.22	1.246076	.67	1.954236	1.12	3.064851
.23	1.258599	.68	1.973876	1.13	3.095654
.24	1.271248	.69	1.993714	1.14	3.126765
.25	1.284025	.70	2.013751	1.15	3.158190
.26	1.296929	.71	2.033990	1.16	3.189930
.27	1.309964	.72	2.054432	1.17	3.221990
.28	1.323129	.73	2.075079	1.18	3.254371
.29	1.336427	.74	2.095934	1.19	3.287078
.30	1.349858	.75	2.116998	1.20	3.320114
.31	1.363424	.76	2.138275	1.21	3.353481
.32	1.377127	.77	2.159765	1.22	3.387184
.33	1.390967	.78	2.181471	1.23	3.421226
.34	1.404947	.79	2.203395	1.24	3.455610
.35	1.419067	.80	2.225539	1.25	3.490340
.36	1.433329	.81	2.247906	1.26	3.525418
.37	1.447734	.82	2.270498	1.27	3.560849
.38	1.462284	.83	2.293317	1.28	3.596636
.39	1.476980	.84	2.316365	1.29	3.632783
.40	1.491824	.85	2.339645	1.30	3.669293
.41	1.506817	.86	2.363159	1.31	3.706170
.42	1.521961	.87	2.386909	1.32	3.743418
.43	1.537257	.88	2.410898	1.33	3.781040
.44	1.552706	.89	2.435128	1.34	3.819040
.45	1.568311	.90	2.459601	1.35	3.857422

TABLE D

PRESENT VALUE INTEREST FACTOR OF $1

n	1%	2%	3%	4%	5%	6%	7%	8%
1	0.990	0.980	0.971	0.962	0.952	0.943	0.935	0.926
2	0.980	0.961	0.943	0.925	0.907	0.890	0.873	0.857
3	0.971	0.942	0.915	0.889	0.864	0.840	0.816	0.794
4	0.961	0.924	0.888	0.855	0.823	0.792	0.763	0.735
5	0.951	0.906	0.863	0.822	0.784	0.747	0.713	0.681
6	0.942	0.888	0.837	0.790	0.746	0.705	0.666	0.630
7	0.933	0.871	0.813	0.760	0.711	0.665	0.623	0.583
8	0.923	0.853	0.789	0.731	0.677	0.627	0.582	0.540
9	0.914	0.837	0.766	0.703	0.645	0.592	0.544	0.500
10	0.905	0.820	0.744	0.676	0.614	0.588	0.508	0.463
11	0.896	0.804	0.722	0.650	0.585	0.527	0.475	0.429
12	0.887	0.789	0.701	0.625	0.557	0.497	0.444	0.397
13	0.879	0.773	0.681	0.601	0.530	0.469	0.415	0.368
14	0.870	0.758	0.661	0.577	0.505	0.442	0.388	0.340
15	0.861	0.743	0.642	0.555	0.481	0.417	0.362	0.315
16	0.853	0.728	0.623	0.534	0.458	0.394	0.339	0.292
17	0.844	0.714	0.605	0.513	0.436	0.371	0.317	0.270
18	0.836	0.700	0.587	0.494	0.416	0.350	0.296	0.250
19	0.828	0.686	0.570	0.475	0.396	0.331	0.277	0.232
20	0.820	0.673	0.554	0.456	0.377	0.312	0.258	0.215
25	0.780	0.610	0.478	0.375	0.295	0.233	0.184	0.146

n	9%	10%	11%	12%	13%	14%	15%	16%
1	0.917	0.909	0.901	0.893	0.885	0.877	0.870	0.862
2	0.842	0.826	0.812	0.797	0.783	0.769	0.756	0.743
3	0.772	0.751	0.731	0.712	0.693	0.675	0.658	0.641
4	0.708	0.683	0.659	0.636	0.613	0.592	0.572	0.552
5	0.650	0.621	0.593	0.567	0.543	0.519	0.497	0.476
6	0.596	0.564	0.535	0.507	0.480	0.456	0.432	0.410
7	0.547	0.513	0.482	0.452	0.425	0.400	0.376	0.354
8	0.502	0.467	0.434	0.404	0.376	0.351	0.327	0.305
9	0.460	0.424	0.391	0.361	0.333	0.308	0.284	0.263
10	0.422	0.386	0.352	0.322	0.295	0.270	0.247	0.227
11	0.388	0.350	0.317	0.287	0.261	0.237	0.215	0.195
12	0.356	0.319	0.286	0.257	0.231	0.208	0.187	0.168
13	0.326	0.290	0.258	0.229	0.204	0.182	0.163	0.145
14	0.299	0.263	0.232	0.205	0.181	0.160	0.141	0.125
15	0.275	0.239	0.209	0.183	0.160	0.140	0.123	0.108
16	0.252	0.218	0.188	0.163	0.141	0.123	0.107	0.093
17	0.231	0.198	0.170	0.146	0.125	0.108	0.093	0.080
18	0.212	0.180	0.153	0.130	0.111	0.095	0.081	0.069
19	0.194	0.164	0.138	0.116	0.098	0.083	0.070	0.060
20	0.178	0.149	0.124	0.104	0.087	0.073	0.061	0.051
25	0.116	0.092	0.074	0.059	0.047	0.038	0.030	0.024

TABLE E

PRESENT VALUE INTEREST FACTOR OF AN ANNUITY OF $1

n	1%	2%	3%	4%	5%	6%	7%	8%
1	0.990	0.980	0.971	0.962	0.952	0.943	0.935	0.926
2	1.970	1.942	1.913	1.886	1.859	1.833	1.808	1.783
3	2.941	2.884	2.829	2.775	2.723	2.673	2.624	2.577
4	3.902	3.808	3.717	3.630	3.546	3.465	3.387	3.312
5	4.853	4.713	4.580	4.452	4.329	4.212	4.100	3.993
6	5.795	5.601	5.417	5.242	5.076	4.917	4.767	4.623
7	6.728	6.472	6.230	6.002	5.786	5.582	5.389	5.206
8	7.652	7.326	7.020	6.733	6.463	6.210	5.971	5.747
9	8.566	8.162	7.786	7.435	7.108	6.802	6.515	6.247
10	9.471	8.983	8.530	8.111	7.722	7.360	7.024	6.710
11	10.368	9.787	9.253	8.760	8.306	7.887	7.499	7.139
12	11.255	10.575	9.954	9.385	8.863	8.384	7.943	7.536
13	12.134	11.348	10.635	9.986	9.394	8.853	8.358	7.904
14	13.004	12.106	11.296	10.563	9.899	9.295	8.745	8.244
15	13.865	12.849	11.938	11.118	10.380	9.712	9.108	8.560
16	14.718	13.578	12.561	11.652	10.838	10.106	9.447	8.851
17	15.562	14.292	13.166	12.166	11.274	10.477	9.763	9.122
18	16.398	14.992	13.754	12.659	11.690	10.828	10.059	9.372
19	17.226	15.679	14.324	13.134	12.085	11.158	10.336	9.604
20	18.046	16.352	14.877	13.590	12.462	11.470	10.594	9.818
25	22.023	19.524	17.413	15.622	14.094	12.784	11.654	10.675

n	9%	10%	11%	12%	13%	14%	15%	16%
1	0.917	0.909	0.901	0.893	0.885	0.877	0.870	0.862
2	1.759	1.736	1.713	1.690	1.668	1.647	1.626	1.605
3	2.531	2.487	2.444	2.402	2.361	2.322	2.283	2.246
4	3.240	3.170	3.102	3.037	2.974	2.914	2.855	2.798
5	3.890	3.791	3.696	3.605	3.517	3.433	3.352	3.274
6	4.486	4.355	4.231	4.111	3.998	3.889	3.784	3.685
7	5.033	4.868	4.712	4.564	4.423	4.288	4.160	4.039
8	5.535	5.335	5.146	4.968	4.799	4.639	4.487	4.344
9	5.995	5.759	5.537	5.328	5.132	4.946	4.772	4.607
10	6.418	6.145	5.889	5.650	5.426	5.216	5.019	4.833
11	6.805	6.495	6.207	5.938	5.687	5.453	5.234	5.029
12	7.161	6.814	6.492	6.194	5.918	5.660	5.421	5.197
13	7.487	7.103	6.750	6.424	6.122	5.842	5.583	5.342
14	7.786	7.367	6.982	6.628	6.302	6.002	5.724	5.468
15	8.061	7.606	7.191	6.811	6.462	6.142	5.847	5.575
16	8.313	7.824	7.379	6.974	6.604	6.265	5.954	5.668
17	8.544	8.022	7.549	7.120	6.729	6.373	6.047	5.749
18	8.756	8.201	7.702	7.250	6.840	6.467	6.128	5.818
19	8.950	8.365	7.839	7.366	6.938	6.550	6.198	5.877
20	9.129	8.514	7.963	7.469	7.025	6.623	6.259	5.929
25	9.823	9.077	8.422	7.843	7.330	6.873	6.464	6.097

TABLE F

NORMAL PROBABILITY DISTRIBUTION

Number of σ from Mean	Area in One Tail	Number of σ from Mean	Area in One Tail
0.00	.5000	1.50	.0668
0.05	.4801	1.55	.0606
0.10	.4602	1.60	.0548
0.15	.4404	1.65	.0495
0.20	.4207	1.70	.0446
0.25	.4013	1.75	.0401
0.30	.3821	1.80	.0359
0.35	.3632	1.85	.0322
0.40	.3446	1.90	.0278
0.45	.3264	1.95	.0256
0.50	.3085	2.00	.0228
0.55	.2912	2.05	.0202
0.60	.2743	2.10	.0179
0.65	.2578	2.15	.0158
0.70	.2420	2.20	.0139
0.75	.2264	2.25	.0122
0.80	.2119	2.30	.0107
0.85	.1977	2.35	.0094
0.90	.1841	2.40	.0082
0.95	.1711	2.45	.0071
1.00	.1577	2.50	.0062
1.05	.1469	2.55	.0054
1.10	.1357	2.60	.0047
1.15	.1251	2.65	.0040
1.20	.1151	2.70	.0035
1.25	.1056	2.75	.0030
1.30	.0968	2.80	.0026
1.35	.0885	2.85	.0022
1.40	.0808	2.90	.0019
1.45	.0735	2.95	.0016
		3.00	.0013

TABLE G

DEPRECIATION SCHEDULE

Depreciable Life of Property Class	Asset Depreciaton Range Midpoint	Depreciation Method	Switch to Straight Line	Half Year Convention
3-year	4 or less	200% D.B.*	yes	yes
5-year	4 to 10	200% D.B.	yes	yes
7-year	10 to 16	200% D.B.	yes	yes
10-year	16 to 20	200% D.B.	yes	yes
15-year	20 to 25	150% D.B.	yes	no
20-year	25 or more	150% D.B.	yes	no
27 1/2-yr	residential rental property	Str. Line	no	no
31 1/2-yr	other real estate	Str. Line	no	no

*Declining Balance

DEPRECIATION PERCENTAGES

Recovery Year	3-Year	5-Year	7-Year	10-Year
1	33.33%	20.00%	14.29%	10.00%
2	44.45	32.00	24.49	18.00
3	14.81	19.20	17.49	14.40
4	7.41	11.52	12.49	11.52
5		11.52	8.93	9.22
6		5.76	8.93	7.37
7			8.92	6.55
8			4.46	6.55
9				6.56
10				6.55
11				3.28